"We all know the powerful allure of lust. Yet, every man can overcome temptation with God's help. This book will allow you to tap into His power to live a pure life."

**Shaun Alexander**
**All-Pro NFL Runningback, Seattle Seahawks**

"The pornographic assault on our culture increases every day. This book will equip you to stand with courage and biblical conviction. I highly recommend it."

**Luis Palau**
**International Evangelist**

"Pornography is a battle every man can overcome. *Think Before You Look* provides forty practical strategies for a winning game plan."

**Patrick Ramsey**
**Quarterback, Washington Redskins**

"*Think Before You Look* is a fresh approach to this age-old problem. I hope every pastor will get this book into the hands of the men in his church. These principles will make a positive and lasting difference."

**Jerry Falwell**
**Chancellor, Liberty University**

"This simple, concise book packs a punch. I have not read a book on the issue of pornography that is so easy to read and is so full of valuable information, resources, and practical help. This is a must read!"

**Craig Gross**
**Founder of XXXchurch.com**

D0721155

"This is an issue that's not going away. Every man needs practical empowerment to win the daily battle. *Think Before You Look* is one of the best resources I've seen."

**David Jeremiah**
**Senior pastor of Shadow Mountain Church–San Diego, California**
**Chancellor of Christian Heritage College**
**Founder of Turning Point Ministries**

"Pornography is a silent, deadly sin among men. It rips the souls of men, and boys, into shreds, invading our thoughts and behaviors. Pornography is an epidemic that should not be ignored by the Church. Daniel Henderson courageously addresses a topic most preachers won't touch, because they may be guilty too. If you or a loved one is seeking to break from the bondage of pornography, this book is a must read and one I recommend."

**Dr. Alan Cureton**
**President, Northwestern College and Radio**

"Every man must read *Think Before You Look* to understand how pornography poisons the human spirit. Pornography is not just a problem, it is a deadly battle for the souls of men. Henderson gives forty powerful reasons to help every man, young and old alike, win the battle before he is hooked in defeat."

**Dr. Elmer Towns**
**Author & Educator**

"This book will be a great encouragement to men and an essential tactical resource for dealing with sexual sin."

**Brandon Cotter**
**Founder/Executive Director**
**purealliance.org**

# DANIEL HENDERSON

# THINK before you LOOK

## Avoiding the Consequences of Secret Temptation

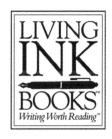

LIVING INK BOOKS
*Writing Worth Reading*™

This book is dedicated to
The Pastor's Prayer Partners,
a group of men who have prayed for me
daily for over a decade.

And to
The S.W.A.T. (Spiritual Warfare Attack Team) Women
who have consistently offered intercession
for my wife and children.

Without your prayers for our purity, protection, prosperity, and provision I would not have the conviction, character, or confidence to write this book. Thank you for blessing our lives with the greatest gift of all—the treasure of your loving and sacrificial intercession.

I also dedicate this project to the memory of my beloved brother and friend, Bob Bridges, whose testimony of renewed love for his wife and courageous commitment to sexual purity inspired so many men.

# Acknowledgments

**M**Y SPECIAL THANKS goes to the hundreds of men who have joined me in extraordinary seasons of renewal at our Prayer Summits over the past decade. Your willingness to participate in these miraculous moments in God's presence has taught me many lessons about repentance, transparency, and genuine transformation.

Of course, my dear wife Rosemary continues to be the treasure of my heart and life. I will always be grateful for her support, patience, and grace.

My children, Justin, Jordan, and Heather, continue to inspire me to integrity, purity, and Christlikeness. Thank you for your loving encouragement and prayers.

Allison Shaw provided extraordinary assistance in research and editing, contributing her skills as a capable librarian.

Dan Penwell and the AMG staff offered tremendous collaboration and guidance throughout the journey of writing this book. It was a delight to work with them.

For more information on Daniel Henderson's ministry or additional resources for personal renewal and congregational revival go to:

www.strategicrenewal.com
www.danielhenderson.org
or
www.pastorsconnection.com

A downloadable "40 Reasons" screen saver and group study guide are available at www.strategicrenewal.com.

# Contents

# CONTENTS

# Foreword

**D**ANIEL HENDERSON is a regular chapel speaker for the NFL. I had the privilege to meet him in this context. His messages are always relevant, encouraging, and direct. I've also enjoyed reading his previous books and appreciate his love for God and commitment to communicating biblical truth to this generation.

That's why I am pleased to support this important project. Pornography is a struggle for so many men. Silence and seclusion will never enable guys to gain lasting victory in this spiritual battle. I appreciate the fact that Daniel is willing to speak out as a man, husband, father, and respected spiritual leader to provide such a relevant and powerful resource.

The growing proliferation of X-rated publications, Web sites, videos, and DVDs threatens to destroy the moral fabric of our lives, families, and society. *Think Before You Look* proposes that pornography has become the ultimate weapon of mass cultural destruction.

In framing a spiritual battle plan, Daniel Henderson advocates that the hardest thing about life is that it is so *daily* and that the hardest thing about the battle against pornography is that it is so hourly. He proposes that the only way to win the battle is one life at time, one day at a time, one hour at a time, one decision at a time, and one thought at a time. I completely agree. That's why I am pleased to commend this book to you.

Daniel's approach is unique in several ways. Unlike many other presentations on the problem of pornography, this one is not designed as a clinical exploration of the psychoanalysis of addiction or a lengthy explanation on the dark-side of family origins. The stories about other men's problem with porn are minimal. Other books offer great resources of this sort, but the mission is different here.

By design, *Think Before You Look* is shorter than most books on the subject. Many men do not have time for a lengthy psychological treatise, so this shorter treatment should alleviate time-constraint concerns.

Perhaps more importantly, the book title does not presume guilt. Most guys do not want to announce their porn problem at the checkout counter. You do not even have to struggle with pornography to benefit from this book. But, if you do struggle, this resource may just become your most treasured companion in the journey to victory.

*Think Before You Look* is designed as a preventive tool. Daniel calls pornography the number one weapon of spiritual and cultural terrorism against the moral fabric of our country. This book will serve as a spiritual counterterrorism weapon designed for rapid deployment. Each chapter is a practical, no-nonsense, thought-provoking jolt of grace and truth to help you make better decisions every day and every hour when faced with the temptations of porn.

It's been said that the most important sexual organ is the mind. We know the most important spiritual weapon is the truth. The most important moment of decision is now.

If you are interested in that kind of battle plan for conquest over lust and its negative consequences, this is your weapon. Use it daily; apply it faithfully; and enjoy the satisfaction of personal, marital, and family victory.

— Trent Dilfer
Super Bowl Champion NFL Quarterback
(2001)

# Preface

**F**OR THE PAST twelve years, hundreds of busy men have set aside their personal digital assistants, golf clubs, garden tools, and television remotes to travel to the rugged, unspoiled beauty of a remote retreat center. They've gathered with Bibles and songbooks in hand. It is a journey into the unexpected—together.

For three days and three nights, they have no agenda but to seek God. No sermons, designed programs, or outlines of events are planned. Yet over the course of the retreat, these earnest followers read hundreds of Bible passages, some privately, many publicly. Hundreds of songs ring out in a spontaneous and mighty a cappella chorus. Typically, a couple of tender communion services mark the weekend.

The most unusual aspect of the Prayer Summit is the small group sessions. In gatherings of twenty to twenty-five, men sit in a circle for worship, Scripture reflection, and prayer. As the truth pierces hearts, brothers begin to open up to one another. Honest, tender confession springs forth as souls are laid bare and lives are made right with God.

Before long, men are weeping over areas of personal failure and habitual sin. The power of God's deliverance is unleashed through the "effectual fervent prayer" of faithful brothers. Hearts are restored. New resolve toward godliness is infused by the power of the Holy Spirit. The groundwork is laid for better marriages, healthier families, and a new zeal for Christian service.

As a pastor, I have never seen an environment so conducive to authentic and lasting spiritual breakthrough. I have watched, wept, and prayed hundreds of times as men are revived in their walk with Christ while, at the same time, being delivered from long-term habitual sin.

Of course, every man has his own struggle. For some, it is bitterness, dishonesty, pride, substance abuse, marital neglect, or spiritual apathy. By far, the most common source of spiritual defeat is the lure of lust. Occasionally, men confess the problem of a vulnerable imagination. For many, it is a regular battle with pornography. Others have given in to full-scale addiction.

I remember one small group session at our first Prayer Summit. Sam sat weeping uncontrollably in front of a couple dozen men. His sobs were intense. He could barely speak. Other men around the circle were moved with tearful compassion as they looked on. Finally, Sam cried out to God with these words:

Dear God, You know my heart and You've seen my ways. I am so sorry. You know that I cannot forget the look in my young daughter's face the day she and her mother left me because of my problem with pornography. What a fool I had been. Yet, in Your grace You saved me and have given me a brand-new life. You brought me a beautiful, godly woman who has been my faithful and devoted mate for ten years. But, here I am again Lord—addicted to this filth. I'm violating my dear wife, filling my marriage with garbage, and ruining my relationship with You.

Oh God, I am so sorry. Please cleanse me. Deliver me, Lord Jesus.

With those words, Sam completely broke down. A handful of men rushed to his side, laid their hands on his shoulders, and prayed passionate prayers of faith to the Great Deliverer. Other men began weeping openly. A few minutes later intercession for Sam subsided and he enjoyed the caring embrace of brothers who vowed to continue in prayer, encouragement, and accountability. You can guess what happened next.

Throughout the afternoon, more men found a safe place to deal with their ugly secrets and painful addiction to pornography. They came in response to the prescription and promise of James 5:16: "Therefore, confess your sins to one another, and pray for one another, so that you may be healed. The effective prayer of a righteous man can accomplish much" (NASB).

Another paraphrase reads: "Make this your common practice: confess your sins to each other and pray for each other so that you can live together whole and healed. The prayer of a person living right with God is something powerful to be reckoned with" (The Message).

Over the past decade, these scenes have reoccurred with countless stories of renewed victory and revitalized marriages. Some men have continued their recovery through small group Bible studies and accountability sessions. The Prayer Summits keep growing as God keeps working. He is glad to do so as long as we are willing to seek Him and be honest about our weaknesses, failures, and sins.

I am moved beyond words when I think of the burden so many men carry as they battle the sex-crazed culture around them. Even more, I am deeply burdened by the consequences that occur in individual lives, families, and churches because of the onslaught of pornography among my Christian brothers.

Most importantly, I am delighted to see hundreds of men choose a better way.

Sam, in the story above, is a new man. He is free, fulfilled, and fruitful in his Christian life. His marriage is better than ever and God is using him to help many other men. That is the power of choosing a better way.

As a result of my experiences with the men of our church and the undeniable evidence of the magnitude of this problem across our nation, I started documenting the destructive consequences of pornography in the life of a Christian man. Next, I transformed the list into positive reasons to avoid the clutches of lust. The list is not a cure-all for the addicted soul. However, when regularly reviewed and deeply contemplated, it serves as a dose of prevention to help men think before they look.

If just one man is turned away from the sting of a single destructive pornographic encounter, the labor will have been well worth it.

*I made a covenant with my eyes*
*not to look with lust upon a young woman. . . .*
*If I have strayed from his pathway,*
*or if my heart has lusted for what my eyes have seen,*
*or if I am guilty of any other sin,*
*then let someone else harvest the crops I have planted,*
*and let all that I have planted be uprooted. . . .*
*That would be better than facing the judgment sent by God.*
*For if the majesty of God opposes me, what hope is there?*
(Job 31:1, 7, 8, 23 NLT)

*Turn my eyes away from worthless things;*
*preserve my life according to your word.*
(Ps. 119:37)

# INTRODUCTION:
## Considering the Consequences

**'LL NEVER FORGET** Jason. He was a handsome, outgoing blond with great talent. During our college days, we traveled as members of a singing team representing our university and ministering on high school campuses. My most vivid memory of Jason was his big toe—actually, the lack of one.

Years earlier, Jason accidentally shot himself in the foot with a shotgun. The incident left a large gap where his big toe and the ball of his foot used to be. It became his signature comedy routine. Often, while swimming in a public pool, he would hoist his foot high in the air and cry out in apparent panic, "A shark! Help, a shark bit me." Many swimmers would be noticeably startled. Those of us who knew him would burst into laughter. The lifeguards were seldom amused.

If you met Jason today and asked why he shot off his toe, his response would be obvious. No young man shoots himself in the foot on purpose.

Jason would also tell you that he would rather still have his toe. He might give you some pointers on gun safety. While he couldn't go back and reverse the tragedy of this gun accident, he could warn others about the consequences of carelessness with a loaded gun.

In so many ways, sexual desire is a loaded gun. When used properly, the fruit can be good and rewarding. When handled carelessly, the results can be tragic.

This book is a tool kit for the proper use and handling of the desires that often stir in your soul. You will discover forty powerful, positive reasons to properly use and deal with those desires. You will receive warnings, based on reliable wisdom, to keep you from shooting yourself in the foot.

## The Danger of Concealed Consequences

I remember sitting in the home of Mom and Pop Smith many years ago in Tacoma, Washington. At the time, I served as part of a young church planting team. Our fledgling ministry reached Darrell, their college-age son. Mom Smith adopted us all as if we were her own children. Pop Smith seldom came to church, but was always kind and generous when we visited his home, which was often.

> This book is a tool kit for the proper use and handling of the desires that often stir in your soul.

Pop Smith worked around asbestos all his life. I can't remember what he did for a living, but it turned out to be a hazardous choice. His lungs were filled with cancer and his body was marked by a variety of obvious tumors. It was a disturbing sight—and a very sad moment for us all as we said our good-byes. Days later, he died.

Just as the "concealed" consequences of asbestos contamination had destroyed his life, so the subtlety of sin takes a huge toll on our spiritual vitality, our emotional well-being, our family relationships, and even our physical survival in some cases.

Several factors make this danger of concealed consequences a particularly treacherous threat from a spiritual standpoint. First, we face an enemy whose calling card reads: "The Father of Lies." He specializes in deceptions of mind and spirit. He is a master at suppressing the real consequences of sinful choices. Remember, he convinced Eve that eating the fruit of the Eden tree was no big deal and that God's promised penalty was not a serious threat.

Adding to our dilemma is the reality that sin is pleasurable, at least for a season (Heb. 11:25). During that brief season, sin sinks its hooks in us and sets us up for a long journey of misery. Of course, sexual sin has a particular appeal because we are sexual creatures, created by God to enjoy this incredible gift within the boundaries of a monogamous relationship with a member of the opposite sex.

These facts help us understand why pornography has become the devil's tool of choice for luring many to a life of destructive consequences. He makes sure that the negative results are shrouded in pleasure and concealed to the undiscerning mind.

This book is designed to help you recognize the dangerous trap, avoid it, and choose a much better course. If you're already in the clutches of pornography's ambush, renewing your mind with these principles will provide some significant escape routes.

## God's Double-Edged Promise

There is another universal spiritual law that comes into play when we are trapped by the allure of pornography. God established this law primarily as an incentive toward wise and positive behavior. But it cuts both ways. If violated, the law can bring great pain. It is simply stated in Galatians 6:7, 8:

> Do not be deceived, God is not mocked; for whatever a man sows, this he will also reap. For the one who sows to his own flesh will from the flesh reap corruption, but the

one who sows to the Spirit will from the Spirit reap eternal life.

Job, the earliest of all books in Scripture, said it just as clearly with these words, "According to what I have seen, those who plow iniquity and those who sow trouble harvest it" (Job 4:8).

> We always reap what we sow, usually more than we sow and always later than we sow.

Solomon's wisdom reiterated the fact that sinful behavior will always bring negative results: "So they shall eat of the fruit of their own way and be satiated with their own devices" (Prov. 1:31). Even a casual reading of chapters 5, 6, and 7 of Proverbs will remind you of the incredible consequences of sexual sin. The wise king repeated this same unchangeable truth later in Proverbs when he wrote, "The wicked earns deceptive wages, but he who sows righteousness gets a true reward" (11:18). This book is a toolkit to help you sow righteousness as you avoid the destructive fruit.

## Sin's Compounding Interest

Another rather frightening factor in the sowing and reaping principle is the truth of compounding results. We always reap what we sow, often more than we sow and always later than we sow.

The apostle Paul wrote, "Now this I say, he who sows sparingly will also reap sparingly, and he who sows bountifully will also reap bountifully" (2 Cor. 9:6 NASB). The deeper pornography and its accompanying habits sink their claws into your lifestyle, the greater the account of negative consequences grows. Eventually, it will all come cashing and crashing in.

God does not play favorites. These universal truisms apply even to the person engaged in secret, "harmless" sins. The all-seeing, all-knowing Lord is one "who will render to each person according to his deeds"—private and public deeds (Rom. 2:6 NASB).

The good news is that our gracious Father gladly and generously rewards the wise man who avoids damaging choices. He loves us and wants to lavish us with His abundance—in our personal life, marriage, and family. The commitments we make every day in avoiding the call of lust bring benefits far beyond the temporary *thrill* of sin.

## The Sudden Dead End

A couple years ago, I was among a group of pastors visiting a massive church in the Dallas area. As we enjoyed a tour of the facilities, we were particularly intrigued with the multi-story education building. The children's classrooms spanned several floors, featuring hallways decorated with beautiful, Disney-like paintings of Bible stories.

One notable attraction was an enclosed interior children's tube slide that curved from the top floor to a large assembly area a couple stories below. Each Sunday, children by the hundreds take the adventure down to Children's Church, where they are delivered into an extravaganza of music, lights, and Bible stories.

Still kids at heart, several of us desired to ride the slide just to see what the journey would entail. Greg, a pastor from Long Beach, decided to go first. The rest of us lined up enthusiastically. He quickly disappeared through the slick tube, howling with glee. Moments later, we heard a loud thump from below. His happy exhilaration suddenly ended as he screamed, "It's closed off."

Here was a dignified pastor, two floors below, stranded at the end of a slippery dark tube, with no option but to climb back up. As you might guess, we roared with laughter for several minutes as we imagined his predicament. Later we learned that he was claustrophobic. While we enjoyed the hilarity of the moment, Greg was really quite traumatized.

> Our gracious God gladly and generously rewards the wise man who avoids damaging choices.

Greg's brief joyride and startling sudden halt is a good illustration of a life encumbered by pornography. At first it looks attractive. It is even entertaining and briefly fulfilling. But there is, without a doubt, a sudden and difficult thud at the end of the road.

There is one difference between Greg's slide ride and our pornography playground. Greg made the leap for pleasure, assuming a happy result. The one who toys with pornography can absolutely count on it: there is a bitter end ahead.

This book is a simple, heartfelt appeal. Don't jump on the ride. There is a better, happier, and more rewarding course. Join me as we discover that path, utilizing forty grace-giving points of powerful and positive reinforcement.

# A Lonely Lust

A man sits alone with a choice before his eyes,
No one else is present as he wrestles with his lies.
A fire smolders once again from deep within his soul;
He can fuel its growing heat or choose to leave it cold.

Passion begins to flow with a force against his will;
Scenes that grip his mind bring the promise of a thrill.
Emotions rage, needs unfold from a weak and lonely heart;
In this very private moment, will he stop or let it start?

A lovely wife, terrific kids have blessed his simple life;
His gracious God and prayerful friends stand by him in the strife.
But out of sight is out of mind in this moment of clear choice;
Even the indwelling Spirit speaks with ever-fading voice.

Images entice his spirit as their beauty pierce his reason;
Setting aside real joy and peace, he indulges for just a season.
More brief and empty now seems the thrill once it is done;
Regret and shame overwhelm as the lies again have won.

He walks away so dirty, feeling lost in his defeat;
Everything he really loves he chose again to cheat.
Full of remorse in this return to the filth of where he's been;
If only he knew how to stop this madness, before it starts again.

—Daniel Henderson

# Avoiding the Consequences of Secret Temptation

# 40

# Powerful Reasons to Avoid Pornography

# I enjoy the pleasure of a love relationship with God.

T**HE GREAT NEED,** destiny, and reward of the human soul is to love and be loved. When someone is secure in the love of another and free to express and experience this deep soul connection in authentic relationship, he is fully alive.

That's why Jesus emphasized the powerful truth that God's great expectation and desire is that we would "love the Lord our God with all our heart, soul, mind and strength" (see Mark 12:30). That's why the Bible tells us over and over again of God's passionate, persistent attraction to us. In response, "we love him because he first loved us" (see 1 John 4:19).

The most costly trade-off for entanglement in sexual sin is the violation of the love relationship God has provided for our good and His glory. We exchange an intimate life-giving fellowship with our loving heavenly Father for a pseudo-relationship with a nameless airbrushed model.

No wonder porn leaves us so empty. In engaging in porn, we turn away from the only relationship that ultimately satisfies and brings value to life. We give ourselves to an empty illusion of a relationship, tossing true fulfillment aside for the short-lived "fulfillment" of lust.

In one of the most memorable stories in sports history, Olympian Eric Liddell ran with unparalleled passion toward the gold medal in the Paris Olympics of 1924. His style was unorthodox, head thrown back and arms flailing. The secret to his speed and passion was captured in his declaration, "When I run I feel His pleasure."

The story of his refusal to run a qualifying heat on a Sunday, thus forfeiting a prime opportunity for a medal, has inspired millions. Of course, he went on to set a world record in the 400-meter dash on a different day, sticking to his convictions.

What made Liddell so distinguished? He was a man who understood that ultimate fulfillment was found in bringing pleasure to the heart of his Creator. This thrill was far beyond the temporary delight of winning an Olympic race. His relationship with God was his ultimate treasure of pleasure. He knew that any compromise of that relationship would be a loss in life, even if it resulted in a temporal win.

The psalmist said it so clearly:

I have set the LORD always before me. Because he is at my right hand, I will not be shaken . . . you have made known to me the path of life; you will fill me with joy in your presence, with eternal pleasures at your right hand" (Ps. 16:8, 11).

When the temptations of pornography call out to our hearts, we must renew our wandering thoughts and fragile emotions with this truth. God has something far more satisfying for us in an authentic, pure, real, and life-changing love relationship with Jesus.

We must set the Lord *always* before us, remembering His path of life, the joy of His presence, and the eternal pleasures He offers. Truly we can say, "When I remain pure, I feel His pleasure, like a proud papa grinning from ear to ear, beaming with pride and joy." I can remind myself that "when I avoid pornography, my love relationship with Him flourishes."

When the image of a Playboy Playmate is staring you down or the forbidden Web pages seem to be calling your name, renew your mind with these words:

THAT WOMAN DOES NOT EVEN KNOW I EXIST. SHE DOES NOT CARE ONE CENT ABOUT MY WELL-BEING. IN FACT, ALL HER DESIGNS FOR ME ARE SELFISH AND DESTRUCTIVE. SHE WILL LOVE ME AND LEAVE ME, USING ME LIKE A FILTHY RAG. WHY SHOULD I GIVE HER THAT POWER? I WILL NOT CHOOSE HER CHARADE OVER THE COMMITMENT OF LOVE I KNOW AND CHERISH FROM MY HEAVENLY FATHER. THE SAVIOR GAVE HIS LIFE TO GIVE ME LIFE SO THAT I MIGHT BE FULFILLED AND EXHILARATED WITH HIS LOVE, NOT HERS.

One porn site operator spoke truthfully about the industry when she said, "Porn comes down to this: we women are exploiting men's weaknesses. You're handing me your credit card. I'm not a victim. I'm exploiting you!"[1] With this in mind, each of us has a choice to make. Do I prefer the exhilaration of the love of God or the exploitation of a pornographer who wants to destroy my life?

Pastor John Piper framed this issue well when he wrote:

The fire of lust's pleasures must be fought with the fire of God's pleasures. If we try to fight the fire of lust with prohibition and the threats alone—even the terrible warnings of Jesus—we will fail. We must fight it with a massive promise of superior happiness. We must swallow up the little flicker of lust's pleasure in the conflagration of holy satisfaction.[2]

The great thinker and author C. S. Lewis made this same point so well:

> If we consider the unblushing promise of reward and the staggering nature of the reward promised in the Gospels, it would seem that our Lord finds our desire not too strong, but too weak. We are halfhearted creatures, fooling about with drink and sex and ambition when infinite joy is offered us, like an ignorant child who wants to go on making mud pies in the slum because he cannot imagine what is meant by the offer of a holiday at the sea. We are far too easily pleased.[3]

In another place, Piper also states, "the greatest hindrance to worship is not that we are a pleasure-seeking people, but that we are willing to settle for such pitiful pleasures."[4]

In *Mere Christianity,* C. S. Lewis reflected, "I find myself having a desire which no evidence in this world can satisfy; the most probable explanation is that I was made for another world."[5]

Personally, I can testify that the great moments of my life have been those occasions when I am fully engaged in the pleasures that emanate from another world—a holy world. All sin is confessed. I pray or worship, alone or with others, with full comprehension of how much the Savior loves and treasures me. I cherish the open, full, and free exchange of holy passion and exhilarating love. This "high" is better than any empty escapade of lust or fleshly pursuit of fading pleasure. One day of this pleasure is better than thousands of any earthly sort (Ps. 84:10).

The seventeenth-century religious philosopher and mathematician Blaise Pascal said there are three kinds of people: those who have sought God and found Him and who are reasonable and happy; those who seek God and have not yet found Him and who are reasonable and unhappy; and those who neither seek God nor find Him and who are unreasonable and unhappy.

To avoid pornography, we must fill our minds with truths that will throttle our lust and rule our emotions in times of temptation. I urge you to be that "reasonable and happy" man as you seek, find, and thoroughly enjoy God, above all else.

I love the way Max Lucado describes the superior love God offers and the satisfaction of soul it brings:

> If God had a refrigerator, your picture would be on it. If He had a wallet, your photo would be in it. He sends you flowers every spring and a sunrise every morning. Whenever you want to talk, He'll listen. He could live anywhere in the universe, and He chose your heart.[6]

That kind of affection and attention is far superior to anything a porn star can offer.

---

### Positive Truth
### Reason #1

Every day I will remember that the pleasure of my love relationship with God is more thrilling and rewarding than the empty ecstasy of pornography.

---

## 2

# I fulfill my true identity
# as a child of God.

**I**MAGINE SITTING at home in the family room. You are relaxing in front of the television. It is a typical weeknight as you settle in for another edition of the nightly news. Suddenly the lead story pictures Osama bin Laden standing proudly on the steps of the Lincoln Memorial in Washington, D.C. Bin Laden is waving an American flag as he proclaims, "I love America. Long live the President of the United States! Freedom of religion for all!"

If you were eating something, you would choke. If you were taking a drink of iced tea, it would be spewed across the room. You would be riveted with shock as the world's most hated terrorist behaved as out of character as anyone could imagine. This kind of scene is tantamount to Carmen Electra advertising a seminar on sexual purity for teenage girls. Or Jerry Falwell providing a prayer of blessing at a Marilyn Manson concert.

No less bizarre is the scene of a devoted follower of Christ indulging in pornographic eroticism in front of a computer screen, television set, or opened magazine. It is a complete contradiction of character and a violation of basic identity.

The Bible says that a true Christ follower is, at his core, a brand-new person (2 Cor. 5:17). The power of the cross has transferred you from darkness to light and transformed you from a sinner to a saint. Scripture presents many pictures to help you understand the new reality of our new man. It explains that you are:

- ◆ bought with a price and belong to God (1 Cor. 6:20)
- ◆ righteous before a holy God (2 Cor. 5:21; Eph. 4:24)
- ◆ a holy temple indwelt by God's Spirit (1 Cor. 3:16)
- ◆ the light of the world and salt of the earth (Matt. 5:13, 14)
- ◆ a citizen of heaven (Phil. 3:20)
- ◆ complete in Christ (Col. 2:10)
- ◆ united with the Lord and one with Him in Spirit (1 Cor. 6:17)
- ◆ God's masterpiece designed to do good works (Eph. 2:10)
- ◆ seated with Christ in the heavenly realm (Eph. 2:6)

The Bible gives many more descriptions concerning our real identity. Author Bill Gillham says that we are "spirit critters in an earth suit."[7] The earth suit is your flesh, which provides the necessary interface you need in this world so the real spirit critter inside can continue to fulfill the earthly mission. The earth suit is supposed to be the mechanism through which the new life is manifested in this fallen world.

> Battles with pornography are a symptom of a man who has temporarily forgotten who he is.

Unfortunately, we often choose to put on a worn-out worldly costume, pretending to belong to this world. As a result, we disguise and discourage the real person inside.

I like to tell my congregation that sin is really a violation of our core identity. Battles with pornography are a symptom of a man who has temporarily forgotten who he is.

This leads us back to our opening scenario. This baffling picture of Osama bin Laden pledging his love and allegiance to the United States is explained. The commentator reveals that you were actually watching an American citizen in a clever bin Laden costume. You were simply witnessing a masquerade.

Every day, lust urges us to put on an old, outdated, and ill-fitting costume. Pornography is the invitation to our own empty masquerade party. Seeking connection, entertainment, and even a brief thrill, we put on a filthy mask and jump into the worldly action.

But remember—it's just not you. It never will be. Stay away from the spoof. You're better than that. Better to the core of who you are.

## Positive Truth
### Reason #2

Every day I will remember to fulfill my true identity in Christ as a child of God and choose to live above the meaningless masquerade of a private porn party.

# 3

# I experience God's provision of empowering grace.

**M**OST OF US have at one time or another thought, "If only I had known back then what I know now, I certainly would have done things differently." A painful reality of life is that we often do not comprehend the consequences of our actions at the time we make certain decisions. If we could only envision the outcomes in advance, life would be a lot easier.

The truth is, God knows the outcome of every choice we make. He looks at our journey from a perspective far different than ours. His sovereign vantage point allows Him to understand the specific ramifications of our every choice. He wants to warn us away from the destructive fruit of pornography. He seeks to persuade us to a higher and better road. Grace is His method and He offers it to you and me every day.

Grace is the powerful and constant reality of the believer. I define grace as God doing for us, in us, and through us what we cannot do for ourselves—through the person and power of Jesus Christ. I like to think of grace as a supernatural intravenous solution constantly hooked up to the heart. It started to flow the moment we turned toward Christ. It supplies His full provision for all we need, regardless of the trial or temptation. Right now, as you read, it is flowing.

The basic formula in this life-giving current is the power of the Holy Spirit, applying the truth of God's word. But the unique application can change based upon your situation.

When a patient is in the hospital, he is often connected to a basic hydrating solution. Depending on the need, the nurse can add a dose of nutrition, antibiotics, painkillers, or other specialized medication.

> God has tailor-made grace for everything we face.

I often say that God has tailor-made grace for everything we face. As a pastor, I've experienced grace for ministry, for marriage, for parenting, and for suffering in a variety of forms. I've watched people receive saving grace, convicting grace, dying grace, and comforting grace. A powerful grace formula is also available for the lustful heart, even when facing strong temptations with pornography.

Paul makes grace so practical in Titus 2:11, 12: "For the grace of God has appeared, bringing salvation to all men, instructing us to deny ungodliness and worldly desires and to live sensibly, righteously and godly in the present age" (NASB).

Think of this as a preventive grace mix that fills the IV with soul warnings and biblical truths. It's all available to you *before* you choose to give in to temptation. Certainly God gives you grace after you sin as you confess your violation and receive restoration. But He earnestly desires that you receive His grace *prior* to the sinful choices. That is plan A.

This Titus passage tells us that because grace is the new reality of our life in Christ, we can learn to deny (disavow or reject) ungodliness and worldly desires. Ungodliness includes any wickedness or impropriety. Worldly desires are described as the "lust of the flesh, the lust of the eyes, and the boastful pride of life" in 1 John 2:16 (NASB). In fact, the word "desire" is defined as a longing for what is forbidden. Sound familiar?

Here's the great news: Grace can keep us from messing up. It clears our lust-fogged head before we sail into sin. It tames our raging desires before our judgment is consumed. Grace opens the door for our way of escape (1 Cor. 10:13). Grace leads us to a better way to live in a journey of reward, wholeness, and joy. This is God's advanced grace that can kick in when pornography calls.

One of the powerful ways this advanced grace works is by illumining one's heart to the truth about sinful decisions. More specifically, grace warns you of the outcomes of your sin. It shows you the bitter end to your lustful wanderings.

My bank advertises an advance for the customer who runs out of money before running out of month. All you have to do is to go online and, for a small fee, you can get some cash in your account ahead of your next paycheck. I've never used it but suppose it would be handy if things were tight.

When you get stuck between the rock of enticement and the hard place of pornography, grace advances you all you need to get through the moment to the other side of the temptation into victory territory.

The Bible regularly promotes the value of thinking ahead and visualizing either the positive or destructive results of our choices as an incentive to good decisions. On the upside, we are reminded over and over of the earthly blessings and eternal rewards of faithful obedience. The downside reminds us that sinful choices lead down a troublesome path.

Going back to Titus 2:11, 12, we learn that grace shows us how to "live sensibly, righteously and godly in this present age" (NASB). That's the timely, positive grace that flows through the spiritual IV. At just the right moment, we receive fresh desire for what is right and good. As we've seen, the flow of empowerment in that IV also warns us to deny ungodliness and worldly longings for things forbidden.

According to the Titus passage, this grace also empowers our heart to focus on "the blessed hope and the appearing of the glory of our great God and Savior, Christ Jesus" rather than living with a shortsighted passion for passing pleasure. Advanced grace draws us to the One who "gave himself for us to redeem us from every lawless deed, and to purify for himself a people for His own possession, zealous for good deeds" (Titus 2:14 NASB). Grace reminds us of who He is, who we really are, and the difference all of this makes in our daily life. As a result, we become eager and able to do what is right, including the avoidance of pornography.

## Positive Truth
## Reason #3

In my weakness I will rely on the strength of His advanced "tailor-made" grace to turn away from ungodly temptations and receive empowerment for right and rewarding choices.

# 4

# I enjoy my spiritual freedom to its fullest.

**N HIS 2003** State of the Union address, President George W. Bush declared, "Americans are a free people who know that freedom is the right of every person and the future of every nation. The liberty we prize is not America's gift to the world; it is God's gift to humanity."

Freedom is God's gift. The ultimate freedom He offers is not political but spiritual. Many Americans who enjoy political freedom are living in spiritual, emotional, relational, and social slavery due to their many addictions. In fact, millions of Americans are slaves to alcohol, drugs, food, shopping, television, and a variety of other activities that hook people into unhealthy and compulsive behavior.

Sexual addiction is constructed with the three building blocks of sexual fantasy, pornography, and masturbation. Some addicts will masturbate up to twenty times a day. Others are fixated on specific behaviors like voyeurism, bestiality, or violent sex.

The bottom line: millions in this land of the free and home of the brave are neither. Many who claim to know Christ are still slaves of their sin.

Jesus said, "You will know the truth and the truth will set you free" (John 8:32). He went on to declare, "I tell you the truth, everyone who sins is a slave to sin. Now a slave has no permanent place in the family, but a son belongs to it forever. So if the Son sets you free, you will be free indeed" (John 8:34–36).

Every believer needs the daily reminder that our identity is not that of a slave but a son. We are free from the penalty and power of sin, but need the daily grace to live in our liberty as we fulfill our identity and enjoy ultimate intimacy with our Lord.

> Don't you know that when you offer yourselves to someone to obey him as slaves, you are slaves to the one whom you obey—whether you are slaves to sin, which leads to death, or to obedience, which leads to righteousness? But thanks be to God that, though you used to be slaves to sin, you wholeheartedly obeyed the form of teaching to which you were entrusted. You have been set free from sin and have become slaves to righteousness (Rom. 6:16–18 NASB).

I will never forget the feeling I had growing up as I walked off my elementary school campus for the last time. After being caged up in a classroom for many long months, I was now free. Free to sleep, to play, and to hang out with friends on lazy summer days. It was truly a euphoric moment.

Millions have known a similar, more powerful exhilaration—the prisoner who walks from his cell after years of incarceration, the POW who is finally flying home to his country and family, an athlete from Afghanistan or Iraq who represents his country in its first appearance in the Olympics, . . . the lust-laden pornographer who finally has the power to turn away from the allure of a steamy image on a screen, a magazine cover, or a prostitute on a street corner. That is freedom.

Freedom is not simply the privilege of doing what you want. Real freedom is the power to do what you should. This leads to the celebration of emancipation.

Of course, we must realistically assess the difficulty of the pathway to freedom. We are in a spiritual battle that rages unseen all around us. Sexual freedom fighters like you are battling upstream in a dirty downstream world.

There is also a physiological struggle. Researchers have discovered that memories associated with moments of sexual arousal get locked into the brain through an adrenal gland hormone called epinephrine. When we are in a pattern of masturbating to pornographic images, the brain associates orgasm with sexual arousal, creating a chemical routine that makes our freedom harder.

But we must know and believe that freedom can be achieved—because it can. It will require time and perseverance in new habits of thought and response. Ultimately, it is only achieved by the supernatural power of God's grace as we surrender to His Spirit and fill our minds with the renewing force of biblical truth. Keeping these forty reasons in mind every day will help you make the right choices one thought, one moment, one day at a time, stepping toward God's promise and provision for your freedom.

> Freedom is not simply the privilege of doing what you want. Real freedom is the power to do what you should.

Novelist Pearl S. Buck wrote, "None who have always been free can understand the terrible fascinating power of the hope of freedom to those who are not free."[8]

Each day, as we turn our eyes away from the ever-present erotic images, battling the chemical rush that seeks to dominate the brain, we cannot forget the "terrible fascinating power of the hope of freedom." It is ours to enjoy. The bondage has been broken. The price for that freedom was paid by the ultimate sacrifice of Jesus on the cross. His resurrection life is now in us to ensure that freedom. Keep your prison doors open and the prison empty. This choice is yours today.

## Positive Truth
## Reason #4

Because I have been set free,
I will enjoy the full privileges and fulfillment of
my emancipation by steering clear of the
self-imposed prison of pornography.

# 5

# I avoid a life pattern of deception.

**O**VER THE CENTURIES, people have believed lies to their own embarrassment, even their own destruction. Here are some better known examples of folks who seemed confused about the facts.

Joseph P. Kennedy, the father of President John, Senator Robert, and Senator Ted Kennedy was once quoted as saying, "I have no political ambition for myself or my children." Who was he kidding?

Ferdinand Foch, the French marshal, was supreme commander of Allied forces during World War I. A few years before the war he said, "Airplanes are interesting toys, but have no military value." He lived to discover otherwise!

Irving Thalberg said to Louis B. Mayer, head of MGM, when he was considering a bid for the screen rights to *Gone with the Wind*, "Forget it, Louis. No Civil War picture ever made a nickel." Boy, was he wrong!

At his inauguration as president in 1857, James Buchanan, anticipating the secession of the Southern states, remarked, "I am the last president of the United States." Good thing he was wrong.

"No matter what happens, the U.S. Navy is not going to be caught napping," Secretary of the Navy Frank Knox announced on December 5, 1941, just two days before the Japanese attacked Pearl Harbor.[9]

These guys all missed reality. Perhaps their assumptions were based on bad information or a flawed gut feeling. Maybe they simply did not want to admit or believe the evidence. In any event, they messed up. How about you? Some of the flawed reasoning of men caught in pornography goes like this:

I'll do it just one more time.
I won't get caught.
It doesn't hurt anyone else.
This doesn't affect any other part of my life.
I can stop doing this at any time.

We must remember one very important truth. Pornography is an incredibly powerful incentive to a lifestyle of lies.

If you possess some pornography, you probably have to hide it. If you look at pornography, you often have to lie about it or cover your tracks. If you enjoy pornography, you've probably convinced yourself that you deserve a little pleasure. You may even believe it is a harmless sin and does not hurt anyone else.

> Pornography is an incredibly powerful incentive to a lifestyle of lies.

Nobody believed that the *Titanic* would sink either. A virtually unseen and obviously underestimated "enemy," the underwater portion of an iceberg, took down the grand ship. The great lie we must avoid is that we can embrace pornography, snuggle close to its bedfellow deception, and not pay some serious consequences.

Psalm 15 is my favorite among all 150. I love the way it portrays the person who really knows God and is going to live a life of security and well-being. At the core of these blessings is this description: "He who walks with integrity, and works righteousness, and speaks truth in his heart" (Ps. 15:2 NASB).

By the inspiration of God's Spirit, David goes to the heart of the matter. He describes the overall lifestyle as a pattern of integrity, a journey where all the pieces fit. This person has his act together. Then, David cuts a bit deeper by noting that a genuine and secure life is comprised of consistently doing the right thing, at the right time, for the right reason.

Then, he gets to the core issue. A person of integrity "speaks the truth in his heart." Working from the outside in, from the general to the specific, this psalm gives us keen insight about the core of moral integrity, spiritual vitality, and lifelong security. A blameless testimony. Right choices. Self-honesty.

Do you want to live as one who really knows God? Do you want a secure, peaceful, and satisfying life? Of course you do. So do I. We must realize that self-honesty erodes dramatically when we are entangled with pornography. We become spiritually phony, constantly insecure, and relationally distant from the friends and loved ones we are deceiving.

Nathaniel Hawthorne said it clearly, "No man, for any considerable period of time, can wear one face to himself and another to the multitude without finally getting bewildered as to which may be the truth."

It has been said that a lie told often enough can eventually be accepted as truth. We must embrace the wonder of the truth that keeps us free so that we will not begin to believe the frequently repeated deceptions of pornography.

I've heard it said that it takes seven new lies to cover up each initial lie. It is a stressful thing to play games with the truth. The internal tumult of trying to keep track of reality versus non-reality is overwhelming. The demand of constant cover-up with others is significant.

David learned this lesson the hard way and wrote about the burden of hidden sin:

When I kept silent, my bones wasted away through my groaning all day long. For day and night your hand was heavy upon me; my strength was sapped as in the heat of summer.

Then I acknowledged my sin to you and did not cover up my iniquity. I said, "I will confess my transgressions to the LORD"—and you forgave the guilt of my sin (Ps. 32:3–5).

But after he freed himself from deception he could say with confidence, "Yes, what joy for those whose record the LORD has cleared of sin, whose lives are lived in complete honesty!" (Ps. 32:2 NLT).

That's why avoiding pornography is so worth it. Complete honesty. A clear conscience. No hiding. No pretending. Incredible joy. Authentic relationships.

In 1850, Hawthorne published *The Scarlet Letter*, a powerful novel centered on the adulterous relationship of Hester Prynne and the highly respected minister, Arthur Dimmesdale. The fallen pastor, remorseful but not ready to face the consequences, asks the question, "What can a ruined soul, like mine, effect towards the redemption of other souls—or a polluted soul, towards their purification?" He describes the misery of standing in his pulpit and seeing the admiration of his people and having to "then look inward, and discern the black reality of what they idolize." Finally he says, "I have laughed, in bitterness and agony of heart, at the contrast between what I seem and what I am! And Satan laughs at it!"[10]

Indeed, we may fool others as we hide our private pornography playgrounds from them. But it's a miserable existence.

The devil and his minions are aware of our activities. More important, God knows all. I've heard it said that our value to God in the public arena is no greater than our character before God in the private places of life.

The great news is that through the constant renewal of our minds in God's truth and the consistent confession of our sin to God, we can live and walk in truth. We can "truth it" in our hearts and live in the liberty of honesty each day.

## Positive Truth
## Reason #5

I will enjoy the peace and prosperity of living in the truth while refusing to carry the heavy load of lies and the depression of deception.

# 6

# I cultivate a soft and sensitive conscience.

**I**N THE CLASSIC Disney film, Pinocchio asks the Blue Fairy how he can become a real boy. She replies, "Prove yourself brave, truthful, and unselfish and someday you will be a real boy. You must learn to choose between right and wrong."

Pinocchio inquires, "Right and wrong? But how will I know?" The Blue Fairy answers, "Your conscience will tell you."

In answer to Pinocchio's naive question about the meaning of "conscience," his friend Jiminy Cricket explains, "Well, I'll tell you. Your conscience is that still small voice that people won't listen to. That's just the trouble with the world today . . ."

Pinocchio asks, "Are you my conscience?"

The Blue Fairy asks Jiminy Cricket if he would like to be Pinocchio's conscience. After he agrees, the Blue Fairy makes this pronouncement, "I dub you Pinocchio's conscience, Lord High Keeper of the Knowledge of Right and Wrong, Counselor in Moments of Temptation and Guide along the Straight and Narrow Path. Now remember Pinocchio, be a good boy and always let your conscience be your guide." The scene culminates with Jiminy Cricket offering a song, imploring Pinocchio to give a whistle when he is in trouble and facing the strong urges of temptation.

Clearly, a soft and tender conscience was elevated in this classic film. *What a far cry from the values being promoted by Hollywood these days!*

I often joke with my wife that the reason I typically fall asleep within sixty seconds of my head hitting the pillow is a clear conscience. While said in jest, we all know that the most peaceful, stress-free life is a life with no spiritual or relational baggage. A clear conscience is good for everyone, whether they fall asleep at lightning speed or not.

> We all know that the most peaceful, stress-free existence is a life with no spiritual or relational baggage. A clear conscience is good for everyone.

"Conscience" literally speaks of a moral awareness. It is the internal faculty that enables us to distinguish between right and wrong. It urges one to do that which he recognizes to be honorable and restrains him from doing that which he recognizes to be immoral. Conscience passes judgment on his acts and executes that judgment within his soul. Our conscience bothers us when we violate it by creating inward disquietude, distress, shame, or remorse. It commends us when we act according to our convictions.

Conscience is innate. Because we are created by God we bear God's image. We are living souls with spiritual capacity and do not need to whistle for Jiminy Cricket to know right from wrong.

According to Romans 2:14, 15, every person has an active conscience although, over time and through blatant disobedience, it can become dulled. It is not the product of the environment, training, habit, or education, though it is influenced by all of these factors. One theologian observed, "Conscience is a gift of God. It is a guardian of morality, justice, and decency in the world. It is an irrefutable testimony to the existence of God."[11]

The apostle Paul's example calls us to a healthy pattern of mental and spiritual hygiene. He said, "So I strive always to keep my conscience clear before God and man" (Acts 24:16). He would later explain to his trusted protégé, Timothy, the importance of a clear conscience: "The goal of this command is love, which comes from a pure heart and a good conscience and a sincere faith" (1 Tim. 1:5). Paul continues in that chapter by noting that those who reject a good conscience eventually shipwreck their faith (Acts 24:19). That's not a good conclusion for anyone's life.

What is the connection between Jiminy Cricket and pornography? What can we learn from Pinocchio about our battle with porn?

A clear conscience always beats a corrupted conscience. Sexual fantasies, pornography, and masturbation violate the conscience. Regular engagement in these avenues of sin can dull and eventually callous the conscience. That road is described in Romans 1. "Furthermore, since they did not think it worthwhile to retain the knowledge of God, he gave them over to a depraved mind, to do what ought not to be done" (Rom. 1:28).

A clear conscience means you are sensitive and responsive to the Holy Spirit. It means you never have to look over your shoulder, wondering what unresolved issue may be following you. It means you never have to walk the other way when you see someone coming because your relationships are out of order. It means God can use you for His purposes on a daily basis.

To enjoy a clear conscience, I must keep short accounts with God and others. Immediate, sincere confession, from a heart of genuine repentance, keeps the conscience clear vertically. Regular maintenance of relationships with others is essential. If I've sinned against someone, I ask forgiveness and make it right. No excuses. No procrastination.

How about this? Next time you are tempted start whistling. Call the tune the "Pinocchio Porn Polka" or the "Conscience Concerto." Of course, this is humorous exaggeration. But do whatever you have to do to remind yourself that you'd rather keep your conscience clear and pliable before the Lord than take one more step down the path of perversion.

## Positive Truth
## Reason #6

I will cultivate a soft and sensitive conscience
through consistent confession of my sin
and a resolve toward authentic purity.

# 7

# I turn away from the solicitation of harlots in my heart.

**A**CTOR HUGH GRANT got caught soliciting oral sex from a prostitute in Los Angeles in 1995. It was rather embarrassing, but in Hollywood, these things are not uncommon.

Dick Morris, adviser to President Clinton, carried on a long-term "business relationship" with call girl Sherry Rowland, paying two hundred dollars an hour for extramarital pleasures. In the summer of 1996, she called a tabloid and received $50,000 to tell the story. Morris was forced to resign the week of Clinton's acceptance speech at the Democratic National Convention.

In 1997, the *Globe* ran photos and stories of the respected husband and sports commentator Frank Gifford with Suzen Johnson. The tabloid reportedly paid the former flight attendant $75,000 to entice Gifford into a hotel room equipped with a hidden video camera.

News reports are regularly sprinkled with twisted stories about high-profile people caught soliciting prostitutes. Admittedly, some accounts are more shocking than others.

Now, here's one to beat them all. Can you imagine the front-page headlines of your town's newspaper announcing to the entire community that over the years you'd had sex with

2,478 prostitutes? Your boss would be enraged. Your coworkers would be horrified. The neighbors would be disgusted. Your wife would be devastated. Your children would be hurt and humiliated beyond words. You'd feel like the scum of the earth. Your reputation and future would be shattered.

> While the news in your hometown may never carry the story of your romps through the red-light district, heaven's headlines report every visit.

Now, I am not trying to make you feel inordinately horrible but, actually, the headline is true. The number of prostitutes may need to be adjusted up or down, but the fact remains. When a man looks at pornography to lust and masturbate, he's just added another harlot to his harem.

The word *pornography* derives from the Greek (*porne*, harlot, and *graphos*, writing). The word now means "1: a description of prostitutes or prostitution 2: a depiction (as in writing or painting) of licentiousness or lewdness: a portrayal of erotic behavior designed to cause sexual excitement."[12]

Now, God does love the souls of porn stars and wants to change them by His gospel of grace. But let's be frank. For all intents and purposes, those women you mentally engage on the page are grimy prostitutes. They've "done it" with more men than you can imagine, not to speak of all the guys who act like they are having sex with them via the porno pix.

In Jesus's day the religious elite believed that as long as you did not physically commit an act of immorality, you were a holy guy. Jesus dismantled that idea in one fell swoop when He pronounced, "You have heard that it was said, 'Do not commit adultery.' But I tell you that anyone who looks at a woman lustfully has already committed adultery with her in his heart" (Matt. 5:27–29).

So, while the headlines in your hometown may never carry the story of your romps through the red-light district, heaven's headlines report every visit. That sure adds a little perspective to your next stopover at the wandering eyes Web page.

### Positive Truth
### Reason #7

Because my life was designed by God for high and holy purposes, I will avoid the red-light district of the heart while cherishing the higher pleasure of purity.

# 8

# I refuse the temptation of idolatry.

**I**F YOU'VE EVER traveled in Third World countries, you've observed a variety of idols concocted by the religion and culture of those peoples. Whether it is a big-bellied Buddha or colorful statue with multiple arms and an elephant head, the sight seems pretty strange to a Westerner.

Here in America, we actually devise a lot more idols than in a foreign country. They just take on different forms. You'll find our idols in television broadcasts, in magazines, and on billboards. They may not seem as abnormal, but they are every bit as troubling. As George Bernard Shaw observed, "The savage bows down to idols of wood and stone; the civilized man to idols of flesh and blood."[13]

An idol is anything that takes the place of God as a source of affection, satisfaction, and pleasure.

We're pretty open about our idols here in America. We have an entire television franchise built around the concept of idol worship. It began as the phenomenon *Pop Idol* over in the United Kingdom. In 2002, *American Idol* arrived on American shores and became an overnight success. With two shows each week, *American Idol's* audience grew consistently, culminating when over thirty million viewers tuned in for the finale. The second season was even more successful, drawing fifty thousand potential contestants. It seems we all want to see an idol, pick an idol, or be an idol. There's a lot of worship going on.

Of course, I do not want to be too hard on all the participants in *American Idol*, because I know some of them are people of faith. But just the title and the rage over the show demonstrate the symptoms of a deep, cultural drift.

> An idol is anything that takes the place of God as a source of affection, satisfaction, and pleasure.

The fact is that *American Idol* is tame compared to the thousands of erotic gods and goddesses worshiped every day in our country through various outlets like strip clubs, adult stores, and X-rated Web pages. Porno-church may be the largest denomination in our country (or should that be the largest "demonization" of our country). Clearly, it is a massive concern.

Why stop the idolatry and stop attending church at the porn altar? For one, God is very clear about the heartache of idolatry.

From the start, He stated in the Ten Commandments:

> You shall have no other gods before me. You shall not make for yourself an idol in the form of anything in heaven above or on the earth beneath or in the waters below. You shall not bow down to them or worship them; for I, the LORD your God, am a jealous God, punishing the children for the sin of the fathers to the third and fourth generation of those who hate me, but showing love to a thousand [generations] of those who love me and keep my commandments (Exod. 20:3–6).

In Ecclesiastes 7:26, He is even more specific:

> And I found that [of all sinful follies none has been so ruinous in seducing one away from God as idolatrous women] more bitter than death is the woman whose heart is snares and nets and whose hands are bands. Whoever pleases God shall escape from her, but the sinner shall be taken by her. (Amplified).

One of the more profound ideas in the Bible is that we eventually become like the object of our worship. We develop a character consistent with our God or gods. (See Ps. 115:4–8; 135:15–18.) We need to choose the objects of our worship very carefully. Our worship determines our destiny.

Remembering the benefits of singular worship of the Lord our God can help us tear down the pornographic altars we have constructed and return to the Lord. I am encouraged by the elderly apostle John's final words in his first epistle:

> We know that we are children of God, and that the whole world is under the control of the evil one. We know also that the Son of God has come and has given us understanding, so that we may know him who is true. And we are in him who is true—even in his Son Jesus Christ. He is the true God and eternal life. Dear children, keep yourselves from idols (1 John 5:19–21).

My take on this verse is: Forget all your idols because you have the astounding privilege of knowing the one true God and His eternal life. He will help you understand the value of your life in Him. Even the Old Testament prophet Jonah encouraged us to a better alternative to idolatry: "Those who cling to worthless idols forfeit the grace that could be theirs" ( Jonah 2:8).

Grace. Intimacy with God through Christ. Knowing, enjoying, and living the truth. These things certainly beat any *American Idol.* Jesus calls us to pure, unadulterated, and exhilarating worship. Let's set our hearts to become like Him, not Hugh Hefner, as we choose to worship at His altar.

## Positive Truth
## Reason #8

I will refuse the temptation of porn-idolatry and set no other "gods" before the one true God who has given me a heart to worship Him alone.

# 9

# I prove to be a faithful
# steward of my money.

**E**VERYBODY SEEMS to care about what we do with our money these days. Merchants and marketers of every kind want a chunk of our change. They bombard our mailboxes with ads. They interrupt our football games with commercials. They even try to disrupt our dinner with annoying phone calls, just to get a piece of the financial action.

Investors and insurance salesmen have a better idea for your hard-earned cash. The IRS wants an accounting for every dollar. The church and thousands of charities could use some of your funds. Of course, the wife has plans for the house and the kids have to go to college. All of these people and many more care about what we do with our money. The question is, do we care?

Buying adult magazines, subscribing to porn Web sites, purchasing X-rated videos, and ordering on-demand television shows all support the most disgusting industry of all time.

Pornography earnings are estimated at $10 billion to $14 billion a year in the United States (the lower figure is according to *Fortune* magazine) and $56 billion worldwide. *Forbes* magazine breaks down the global profits this way: adult videos, $20 billion; sex clubs, $5 billion; magazines, $7.5 billion; phone sex, $4.5 billion; escort services, $11 billion; cable, satellite, and pay-per-view TV, $2.5 billion; CD-ROMs and DVD ROMs, $1.5 billion; Internet (sales and memberships), $1.5 billion; novelties, $1 billion; and others, $1.5 billion.[14]

According to the statistics, porn revenue is larger than combined profits of all professional football, baseball, and basketball franchises in the United States and exceeds the combined incomes of ABC, CBS, and NBC ($6.2 billion).[15] Child pornography alone generates $3 billion annually and the average age of a person's first Internet exposure to pornography is eleven. Figures revealed nearly 90 percent of children ages eight to sixteen who have access to the Internet have viewed pornographic sites while doing their homework.[16]

The battle to counteract porn is another extension of the price tag for sex selling in our culture. America Online blocks 2.4 billion adult-oriented messages per day, which accounts for 80 percent of all incoming e-mail. Businesses spent approximately $200 million on anti-spam protection in 2003. Lost productivity in U.S. organizations due to spam accounted for up to $10 billion in 2003.[17] The majority of spam is porn-related.

And think of the price tag associated with the criminal activity directly related to pornography. Consider the arrests of child pornographers, rapists, pedophiles, and voyeurs. Experts agree that porn serves as a how-to guide for sex crimes, particularly the molestation of children. Research has demonstrated that sexually-oriented businesses, such as strip clubs and massage parlors, attract crime to communities. Land use studies by the National Law Center for Children & Families concur. This organization demonstrated that Phoenix, Arizona, neighborhoods where adult businesses were located experienced a 506 percent higher number of sex offenses than areas without porn businesses. In those same neighborhoods, property crimes were 43 percent greater and violent crimes 4 percent higher.[18]

Add to this the multiplied millions of dollars spent in prevention and treatment programs for sexual addiction and other severe behavioral perversions directly linked to the onslaught of porn in our culture.

As if this is not enough, think of the human cost of broken marriages, shattered homes, scarred children, and dysfunctional citizens, all because of the vise grip of pornography.

My friend Steve got hooked on Internet pornography. As the credit card bills amassed, he felt he needed more. He met a lady from Eastern Europe on the Internet and began a cyber affair with her. Eventually he traveled to her country for some sexual adventure, still spending money on Internet porn. Finally, his wife confronted him. The total financial price tag amounted to over $225,000. The human price tag was incalculable.

Through extraordinary amounts of prayerful support from friends, the family finally reconciled. Steve and his wife attended counseling and they've since relocated to another town to get a fresh start on life. But the scars will always follow them and they'll be digging out of debt for years. We all pray they make it.

Think of the billions of dollars resulting in millions of broken lives. I find myself wondering what that money could do if channeled to causes like providing job training for the poor, education for under-

> Pornographers care what we do with our money. So, let's consider. How much of our hard-earned cash do we want to invest in this industry?

privileged children, after-school programs for students, or funding for various church and charity initiatives. I know this may be an unrealistic ideal, but if more of us would think before we look and pray before we pay, we might start turning the tide.

Believe me, pornographers care what we do with our money. So, let's consider. How much of our hard-earned cash do we want to invest in this industry? A dollar? A few hundred? Thousands? I say, NOT ONE CENT.

We are stewards of every hard-earned penny because ultimately the Lord owns it all. May He give us care and conviction about what we do with His funds. As Proverbs 3:9 reminds us, "Honor God with everything you own; give him the first and the best" (The Message).

This is worth thinking about next time you are tempted to look up and pay up for porn.

---

## Positive Truth
## Reason #9

I will endeavor to be a faithful steward of my money,
using my hard-earned funds to build up
my life and my world, not destroy.

# 10

# I prove to be a faithful steward of my time.

**T SEEMS THE** primary commodity in our society has shifted from money to time. Time has become the greatest gift we can give another and the most prized possession we must guard. This then presents another great reason to avoid the enticement of pornography. Consider some facts about wasted time.

In a study by Stanford University, researchers found that 49 percent of those who responded spent one to five hours a week on the Internet. Another 14 percent of the respondents spent more than ten hours a week on the Internet while 22 percent said they spent between five and ten hours a week with mouse in hand.[19]

In 2001 the UCLA Center for Communication Policy revealed that 60.7 percent of employees surveyed said they visit Web sites or surf for personal use at work (up from 50.7 percent in 2000).[20] Andy Mindel of Wordtracker.com notes that the top keyword searches on the Internet are typically "sex," "mp3," and "hotmail."[21]

One of the telling conclusions of this research is that Web surfers are becoming socially isolated from family and friends. The Stanford researcher noted, "Life becomes a continuous stream organized around the Internet." The Stanford report comes two years after a similar but smaller study at Carnegie Mellon University warning that Web users were more inclined to be lonely or depressed.

For our purposes, it is not hard to conclude that any fascination with Internet porn amounts to a miserable squandering of precious time and takes away from things substantially more meaningful in life.

Of course, the Internet is not the only black hole of time consumption. Consider the hours we might waste watching racy movies or adult videos. Think about times squandered perusing steamy magazines, lingerie catalogs, or other printed images that turn us on.

It's a bit raw to say it this way, but consider the amount of time a guy may spend over a lifetime getting aroused and masturbating. Would it amount to 24 hours or 240? Maybe more, maybe much more. To be specific, let's say a guy views some porn and masturbates twice a week and it takes 10 minutes for each episode. That's 1,040 minutes, or 17.3 hours a year. Think of what could have been done with that time. More importantly, think of the opportunities to connect with real people that may have been missed.

> Any fascination with Internet porn amounts to a miserable squandering of precious time and takes away from things substantially more meaningful in life.

The great thing about omitting masturbation from your schedule and letting the natural process of nocturnal emissions occur is that you aren't wasting a bit of time, because it occurs in your sleep.

Of course, there is no point groveling in guilt. But there is great value in reaching deep for new resolve to be a good and godly steward of the gift of time.

In my first book, *The Seven Most Important Questions You'll Ever Answer*, I spoke of the importance of time. I explained the two ideas on time as presented in the Bible. The first is the idea of *chronos*, a Greek term that means time measured in minutes, hours, days, and years. The other is captured in the word *kairos*, which addresses moments and seasons of opportunity. I reminded readers that our goal is to discover "*kairos* in the chaos of our *chronos*."[22]

How many people might I minister to this year with an extra 17.3 hours? How many lives might be touched or changed as I embrace the stewardship of my minutes and my moments?

Here's a little additional inspiration. Moses prayed, "Teach us to number our days aright, that we may gain a heart of wisdom" (Ps. 90:12). The apostle Paul encourages our hearts with these words, "Therefore be careful how you walk, not as unwise men but as wise, making the most of your time [*kairos*], because the days are evil" (Eph. 5:15, 16 NASB). James 4:14 states, "Yet you do not know what your life will be like tomorrow. You are just a vapor that appears for a little while and then vanishes away" (NASB).

Benjamin Franklin urged, "Dost thou love life? Then do not squander time, for that's the stuff life is made of." When I wrote about time in my first book, I quoted this wonderful piece of poetry. It is still one of my favorites.

When as a child I laughed and wept,
Time crept.
When as a youth I waxed more bold,
Time strolled.
When I became a full-grown man,
Time ran.
When older still I daily grew,
Time flew.
Soon I shall find, in passing on,
Time gone.[23]

I must treasure every minute because eternity is in it. What a powerful incentive to avoid the time waster of porn. I can invest my time and life so much more strategically and wisely. I can give more of myself to my wife, family, and friends. I can carve out more opportunities for ministry and service. Others will be blessed. I will feel better. And eternity will reward me for my stewardship.

## Positive Truth
## Reason #10

I will prove to be a wise steward of the limited commodity and valuable treasure of time as I use it to enhance healthy relationships, not tear them down.

# 11

# I abstain from any promotion and support of the pornography industry.

**I**MAGINE ARRIVING home one afternoon to open a letter from the Al Qaeda terrorist network, thanking you for your generous and regular support for its worldwide terrorism efforts. The letter gratefully acknowledges your consistent endorsement of the network's efforts through your use of its products, your promotion of its propaganda, and the time and money you have devoted to its cause. The letter even includes a line about your willingness to avoid "making waves" as the terrorists systematically spread their networks into the culture.

I am sure you would be enraged—and hopeful that the FBI is not monitoring your mail. Of course, no freedom-loving American in his right mind would support global terrorism.

But, in reality, the pornography industry is the most powerful network of spiritual, moral, and cultural terrorists in the world. The devastation they generate in hearts, homes, families, and society is unprecedented and very scary.

Consider the growth of this network of moral terrorism. In 1998, there were 14 million pornographic Web pages indexed by Google; in 2003, there were 260 million—an increase of

1,800 percent. The Kaiser Family Foundation found in a 2001 poll that 70 percent of fifteen- to seventeen-year-olds had accidentally stumbled across pornography online.[24]

There are also over 100,000 Web sites offering illegal child pornography and 89 percent of them make sexual solicitations of youth. Seventy-two million people visit pornographic Web sites worldwide annually.

Traffic measurements from Hitwise found that, not surprisingly, males represented 65 percent of visitors to the sites in the U.S. adult category (which includes all forms of adult erotica and X-rated sites) during August 2003. The average session time was just under five minutes.

Nearly 72 percent access the explicit sites at home while 28 percent dare to view the content in the workplace.[25]

What tactics are being utilized in the spread of this morally repulsive network? The National Research Council (NRC) found in the landmark study *Youth, Pornography and the Internet* that

> The pornography industry is the most powerful network of spiritual, moral, and cultural terrorists in the world.

"The revenue models of the adult online industry suggest that broad exposure is needed to attract potential customers, and so the industry engages in tactics that seek to generate the broadest possible audience."

According to one study, large numbers of minors are exposed to the sea of pornography. Many of these minors may stumble onto these sites through "porn-napped" and "typosquatted" Web sites.[26]

Porn-napped sites are expired domain names of innocent sites that are taken over by pornographers. Typosquat Web sites are those where an unscrupulous pornographer has deliberately registered names with typos to drive unknowing customers to pornography sites.

The porn network is utilizing mainstream hotel chains like Marriott, Westin, and Hilton to disseminate their smut. These chains all offer in-room X-rated movies delivered to the hotel by one of two major distribution companies, LodgeNet or On Command. Some analysts say these in-room sex movies generate more money for the hotel chains than revenue from the hotels' minibars.

"The 5 percent or 10 percent of revenue that the hotel chain gets, that's pure profit to them because they have no cost," says Dennis McAlpine, an entertainment industry analyst. "They didn't put in the wiring system, they didn't supply the programming." [27]

They profit; the pornographers prosper; our culture decays; and your family suffers. General Motors Corporation at one time owned the national satellite distribution service DirecTV, that channels pornography into millions of American homes for a nice profit. Though General Motors sold its stake in DirecTV to Rupert Murdoch's News Corporation, the satellite network continues to offer pornography channels.

We will never forget the horrifying images of 9/11. The tragic loss of life, the collapse of the World Trade Center's Twin Towers, a gaping hole in the Pentagon, the smoldering ashes in a Pennsylvania field, and the realization that our borders are no longer safe from unexpected and costly assaults still cause us to tremble.

While it is not as visible or distinct, the pornography industry is terrorizing our culture, heaping massive doses of destruction on us all. Granted, we are doing it to ourselves, but if we do not expose the network that facilitates the terror and make clear choices to cut off the support, we will be decimated in a generation.

A publication by the Family Research Council assessed the damage in this way:

The cost of all this in terms of damage to individuals, marriages, and families is incalculable. Research indicates that pornography leads men to view women as little more than objects to be used for sexual gratification. Impossibly "perfect" airbrushed images create unrealistic expectations in young men that hinder them from focusing on more important qualities in a prospective wife. Inundated by the inexhaustible availability of "eager and willing" cybersex partners, married men find it difficult to devote themselves wholly to their spouses. Families suffer when internet porn robs wives and children of precious time that should be rightly spent with them.[28]

While radical Middle Eastern groups are spreading religious, racial, and political terror, the United States is exporting moral and sexual terror.

I remember visiting with a pastor in Romania as we toured the gargantuan palace and nondescript grave of the former dictator Ceausescu. The pastor rejoiced in the political emancipation of his nation and the freedom of worship, once restricted by Communism. Then, with a distressing frown he said, "Now the Christians of Romania are fighting a worse enemy. It is being exported to us from the United States and it is more poisonous than Communism. It is X-rated entertainment." I will never forget that moment. I felt such sadness and shame as I apologized for my country and pledged my prayers for these dear believers.

One final illustration puts the battle in perspective with a more current application. The observation addresses a documentary about Abu Ghraib, the infamous Iraqi prison run by the American military. John Patterson, a writer for London's *Guardian* newspaper, wrote:

Among the images from Abu Ghraib and elsewhere that still remain unseen by the public, there are the dread echoes of American hardcore pornography, particularly of bondage and sadism: a man forced to simulate masturbation near another prisoner's mouth, rumors of the rape of women prisoners by U.S. servicemen, the predominance of humiliating (and to Muslims, deeply blasphemous) nudity everywhere. As Seymour Hersh, the investigator who uncovered this whole sorry story, has pointed out, the result of all this is that the Arab world now thinks of America as a perverted, genitally fixated society exporting its ideas about sex to a devout Iraq.[29]

This is just another poisonous fruit springing from the images and influence of the pornography industry. These are the behaviors of a generation raised on porn.

So, why did I take so much time to expose these facts and acts associated with pornography? Because I never want to get a letter from *anyone* congratulating me for my support of moral terrorism. This is worth thinking about every time I turn on my computer, consider a movie rental, look at a magazine rack, or surf the television channels.

---

### Positive Truth
### Reason #11

As I avoid all promotion and support of the pornography industry, I will discourage its growth and steer clear of its devastation.

---

# 12

# I preserve God's gift of loving sexual expression for its intended purpose.

RAQ'S NATIONAL Museum of Antiquities contained some of the oldest and rarest artifacts in the world. Days before Saddam Hussein's fall, Iraqi forces turned the museum into a military outpost. By the time American forces arrived, the museum had been vandalized. Storerooms were pillaged, decades of research documents burned, ceramic and cuneiform rarities smashed and trampled to pieces. Experts called it a cultural atrocity.

In the cultural war for decency, pornography has set up military operations in the homes and hearts of Americans. The treasures of sexual purity, relational intimacy, and wholesome living have been trashed and trampled underfoot.

Richard Foster made this observation about God's design for the treasury of sexuality:

> Our human sexuality, our maleness and femaleness, is not just an accidental arrangement of the human species, not just a convenient way to keep the human race going. No, it is at the center of our true humanity. We exist, as male and female, in relationship. Our sexualness, our

capacity to love and be loved, is intimately related to our creation in the image of God. What a high view of human sexuality![30]

Obviously, sex was God's idea. It was intended as one of the finest of His gifts to humanity. The enjoyment, the intimacy, and the beauty of it are to be treasured. But our increasingly pornographic society is teaching us to trash the original plan.

The story is told of a young man who left the old country and sailed to America to make a new life in the New World. His parents gave him a meager sum of money and a small box of food as they engaged in a tearful good-bye.

The young man shared a tiny cabin with several others throughout the month-long voyage to New York. At evening time, he carefully ate small portions of his boxed food. From his location he was able to observe the other passengers in the large dining room, chatting and laughing as they enjoyed plates filled with hot, steaming food.

The days went by slowly, and the young man's box of food quickly dwindled. He knew the meals offered in the dining room were certain to cost a lot. He would need that money later.

He began to eat alone in his cabin because the smell from the dining hall made his stomach wrench with hunger. He was down to a few crackers and some moldy cheese each day, drinking tepid rainwater he'd collected in a can.

Three days out of New York, the last of the food was gone except for a wormy apple. Pale, weak, and desperate, he asked the porter in broken English, "How much?" The porter looked confused. "Food," the young man said as he held out some coins and pointed to the dining room. "How much?"

The porter understood. Closing the young man's hands back around his money, he declared, "There is no charge for the food. It was all included in the price of the passage."[31]

Sex within God's boundaries is a feast he has provided as part of the earthly journey. Sadly, many of us have become conditioned to believe that we must eat alone in the secret cubicle of pornography. We become spiritually malnourished and socially isolated as we indulge in the moldy morsels of empty images.

Pornography is designed to arouse a man's desire for a woman's attractiveness and attention, without the rightful price tag for that kind of relationship. In the real world, intimacy and deep romance requires the effort of gaining her heartfelt admiration and winning her affection. This is why porn can become a cheap and empty substitute for the necessary demands of true, meaningful, loving relationships.

> We become spiritually malnourished and socially isolated as we indulge in the moldy morsels of empty images.

Harry Schaumburg, a respected counselor specializing in sexual addiction, notes that a compulsion involving pornography is a by-product of loneliness, pain, the self-centered demand to be loved and accepted regardless of the consequences, and a loss of vital relationship with God.[32]

Sex without love is an empty experience. Self-serving sexual habits pervert the treasure God offers us. Pornography makes this treasure meaningless, trampling it underfoot like the valuables in the Iraqi museum.

I am not a handyman and really don't have much of a collection of tools. But I know enough to know that you do not use a paintbrush to sink a nail. You do not use a hammer to install a light fixture. You do not use a screwdriver to paint the wall.

If we are smart enough to understand the purpose of certain hardware and tools, we certainly can comprehend and cherish the unique function of sex. To do otherwise would be tantamount to demolishing a house by using the wrong tools on the wrong jobs. Your life is more important than a house. Use the right tools for the right purposes as you build it.

## Positive Truth
## Reason #12

As I preserve God's gift of loving sexual expression for its intended God-honoring and wholesome purpose, I guard this treasure for the fulfillment of His plan for my life.

# 13

# I protect the purity and power of my God-given imagination.

**W**HATEVER YOU DO right now, do not picture a green elephant with a purple trunk. Do not think of a two-inch clown jumping up and down on the table in front of where you are sitting. Do not imagine the president wearing a set of Mickey Mouse ears.

Oops. You did it, didn't you? At least for a brief moment. Just the suggestion of a bizarre scene activates the power of the imagination, even when you try not to use it.

God has entrusted each of us with a powerful tool. This tool of imagination has been used for good throughout the centuries. The ability to create beautiful and inspiring images has been a primary ingredient in the world's best paintings, musical scores, architectural feats, hit movies, and technological advances. Every great work is first imagined in the human mind. Michelangelo declared, "I saw the angel in the marble and carved until I set him free."

Author Laurie Hall writes:

> Imagination is the gateway to the soul. The soul is the thinking, willing, and feeling part of us. Imagination exercises the mind, disciplines the will and thrills the emotions. Imagination feeds the soul by driving it to create

something out of nothing. What we imagine becomes what we do.[33]

Unfortunately, many evil and destructive experiences have also incubated and emerged from the human imagination. Sin has infected every imagination and caused this powerful tool to concoct corruption and dish out devastation. As Genesis 8:21 states, "the imagination of man's heart is evil from his youth" (NKJV).

The pornography industry has gained a huge foothold in the commodity of the imagination. Steamy photographs, adult movies, and X-rated Internet sites leave a vivid imprint in the hard drive of the mind. These images are like a "cookie" that is left embedded on your computer after you visit a certain Web site. The information stays in your system just in case you decide to visit that location in cyberspace again. Each pornographic encounter leaves traces of erotic data in your mind for use at some future moment of weakness or temptation.

> "Imagination is the gateway to the soul."

Even without an alluring image right in front of you, lust can be enticed by the memory of the scene from a steamy movie or a romantic encounter from the past. Sadly, this tool of the imagination can be used against you, rather than for you.

What can you do about an infected imagination? Thankfully, there is hope. Just as the computer industry now creates software that removes unwanted files and washes the drive of your computer from various kinds of junk, so the Lord can apply His amazing power to your imagination to give you a fresh start.

First, ask God to cleanse your mind. Confess this area of failure and admit to the porno cookies that are hiding out in the recesses of your inner being. He will cleanse your thoughts by the power of His shed blood.

You can also make a fresh commitment of your mind to the Lord. Through your times of prayer and moments in His Word, dedicate your thoughts and imaginations to God. Let the pure "washing with water, through the word" (Eph. 5:26) scrub and rinse your mental hard drive from those images of impurity.

Replace old files with the reliable and incredibly powerful downloads of biblical truth. Memorize some key passages of Scripture about God's holiness, the call to purity, or the power of the Bible to keep you from temptation.

Stay alert with these memorized verses through a daily review. Keep them at hand at all times. When Satan launched a wilderness assault on the mind, heart, and imagination of Jesus, the Lord pulled out the big guns. (See Matt. 4:1–11.) Even though He was physically exhausted and emotionally weary, He overcame the attack of unholy images and sinful potentialities with the simple statement, "It is written . . ." He was armed and ready with the truth that sets men free and fills their imaginations with nobility.

Finally, let your imagination soar each day in the path of its divine design. The Creator lives in you through His Son Jesus. The One who thought and spoke the galaxies into place wants to nourish your mind. The One who created multiplied thousands of species of animals, birds, fish, plants, and flowers is eager to reshape and renew your capacity to think and dream. Let the purity and beauty of His original design for your mind soar each day as you bask in the astounding diversity and wonder of His creation. Take another step and imagine the love of the Savior on the cross. Imagine the power of His resurrection. Imagine the glories of heaven and the unspeakable joy of your eternal rewards.

Take time each day to defend your mind and maximize your imagination for your good and His glory. Commit to dream of better things, just as Jesus did.

## Positive Truth
## Reason #13

As I protect the purity and power of my God-given imagination, my thoughts will be employed for greater positive, creative life-giving purposes.

# 14

# I develop disciplined character.

**S**ELF-DISCIPLINE is a character quality that shows up in generally proportionate levels in every dimension of life. It is rare to find a physically slovenly person who is disciplined in financial management. A person who can discipline sexual appetites is usually able to control other areas of life. When I master the urges of immediate gratification stimulated by lust, I am on the road to a new freedom in virtually every area of life.

President Theodore Roosevelt explained the value of discipline with these words:

> The one quality which sets one man apart from another—
> the key which lifts one to every aspiration while others are
> caught up in the mire of mediocrity is not talent, educa-
> tion, nor intellectual brightness. It is self-discipline. With
> self-discipline, all things are possible. Without it, even the
> simplest goal can seem like the impossible dream.

I like to define discipline as regulating one's conduct by principle rather than impulse, emotion, pressure, or convenience. It is the ability to delay immediate gratification for worthwhile, long-term goal achievement.

In his book, *Good to Great*, business expert Jim Collins presents his extensive research on the qualities that have caused certain leaders and companies to emerge to greatness. One out-standing characteristic is a commitment to discipline.

To illustrate the essence of this trait, Collins tells the story of a world-class athlete named Dave Scott, who won the Hawaii Ironman Triathlon six times. Scott's daily training regimen included a seventy-five-mile bike ride, twenty-thousand-meter swim, and a seventeen-mile run. Scott believed that a low-fat, high-carbohydrate diet would give him an extra edge. Even though he burned at least five thousand calories a day in train-ing, he would literally rinse his cottage cheese to get the extra fat off. This unusual habit was simply one more small step that he believed would make

> When I master the urges of immediate gratifica-tion stimulated by lust, I am on the road to a new freedom in virtually every area of life.

him just that much better, one more small step added to all the other small steps to create a consistent program of super-discipline.

Collins observed:

> I've always pictured Dave Scott running the 26 miles of the marathon—hammering away in hundred-degree heat on the black, baked lava fields of the Kona coast after swimming 2.4 miles in the ocean and cycling 112 miles against ferocious crosswinds—and thinking to himself: "Compared to rinsing my cottage cheese every day, this just isn't that bad."

Collins' point was that "the good-to-great companies became like Dave Scott. Much of the answer to the question of good to great lies in the discipline to do whatever it takes to become the best within carefully selected arenas and then to seek continual improvement from there. It's really just that simple. And it's really just that difficult."[34]

Researchers in the famed Stanford University "marshmallow study" offered hungry four-year-olds a marshmallow, but told them that if they could wait for the experimenter to return after running an errand, they could have two marshmallows. As expected, some followed their impulses and gobbled the marshmallow right away when the facilitator departed. Others waited a few minutes while some delayed gratification until the researcher returned fifteen or twenty minutes later.

Years later when the children graduated from high school, Stanford researchers were still evaluating them. The differences were dramatic. The resisters were more positive, self-motivated, and persistent in the face of difficulties because they were able to delay gratification in pursuit of their goals. They had the habits of successful people which resulted in more successful marriages, higher incomes, greater career satisfaction, better health, and more fulfilling lives than most of the population.

Those who submitted to the enticement of the marshmallow earlier were more troubled, stubborn and indecisive, mistrustful, and less self-confident. They still could not put off gratification. They had trouble subordinating immediate impulses to achieve long-range goals. When it was time to study for the big test, they tended to get distracted into doing activities that brought instant gratification. This impulse followed them throughout their lives and resulted in unsuccessful marriages, low job satisfaction and income, bad health, and frustrating lives.[35]

Every time you see a nude image or are tempted to fantasize over an attractive woman, think "Marshmallows!" The power to make a disciplined choice will turn into useful restraint for daily living in many other areas of your journey.

Galatians 5:22 reminds us that self-discipline is a characteristic of the Holy Spirit and can be a regular fruit of our lifestyle. Paul wrote to the emotionally fragile Timothy, reminding him that God had given him a spirit of self-discipline to overcome his counterproductive impulses (2 Tim. 1:7). Paul also spoke candidly of his own determined pursuit of self-discipline when he wrote:

> Do you not know that in a race all the runners run, but only one gets the prize? Run in such a way as to get the prize. Everyone who competes in the games goes into strict training. They do it to get a crown that will not last; but we do it to get a crown that will last forever. Therefore I do not run like a man running aimlessly; I do not fight like a man beating the air. No, I beat my body and make it my slave so that after I have preached to others, I myself will not be disqualified for the prize (1 Cor. 9:24–27).

Richard Foster writes:

> Sex is like a great river that is rich and deep and good as long as it stays within its proper channel. The moment a river overflows its banks, it becomes destructive, and the moment sex overflows its God-given banks, it too becomes destructive. Our task is to define as clearly as possible the boundaries placed upon our sexuality and to do all within our power to direct our sexual response into the deep, rich current.[36]

The Bible defines the banks for the river. The Spirit gives us power to direct our sexual response.

When a person makes foolish choices to let the river of desire run wild, they will reap a flood of anguish and regret. With daily choices of Spirit-empowered discipline, a man will do well and reap the blessings of a healthy, wholesome lifestyle.

One of Aesop's fables tells of a man and his wife who had the good fortune to possess a goose that laid a golden egg every day. They soon began to think they were not getting rich fast enough and, imagining the bird must be made of gold inside, they decided to kill it to secure the whole store of precious metal at once. But when they cut it open, they found it was just like any other goose. Thus, they neither got rich all at once, as they had hoped, nor enjoyed any longer the daily addition to their wealth.[37]

Self-discipline is a daily addition to the wealth of your life. Stick with it. Do not become impatient with its benefit by destroying its blessings.

Think before you look and make the choice for self-restraint. Little by little this commitment will have a profoundly positive impact on your life as you resist the marshmallow of masturbation and lust.

## Positive Truth
## Reason #14

By conquering the temptations of pornography, I will develop the blessings of disciplined character with positive results in every area of my life.

# 15

# I guard the integrity of my Christian testimony.

NE OF THE more disturbing principles in life is that it takes much longer to build something of worth than to destroy it.

A positive illustration of this occurred on August 18, 2003, when a twenty-four-year-old woman from China tipped over 303,621 dominos, breaking a nineteen-year-old record for the world's longest solo domino topple. Ma Lihua said she put in thirteen-hour days for nearly seven weeks. That's 637 hours or 26.5 days to create the domino design. It took just over four minutes to knock down the series of white, red, and yellow tiles that revealed the words "World Record" and images of electrical appliances.[38]

A well-known negative example was the *Titanic*, one of the largest and most luxurious ships in the world. It had a gross carrying capacity of 46,329 tons. The ship was 882.5 feet long and 92.5 feet wide at its widest point. This nautical masterpiece consumed construction crews and artisans of all kinds for three years. From the time of impact with the submerged iceberg on its maiden voyage, the ship took two hours and twenty minutes to sink and perhaps another six minutes to travel the two miles to the ocean floor. Thousands of years of human life expired in those moments as about fifteen hundred passengers and ship personnel perished.

How long does it take to establish an honorable Christian testimony? Many years of prayer, sweat, and tears. How long does it take to destroy all that you have built? Minutes. It's always that way. We establish our integrity over many years of law-abiding, self-restrained, family-oriented behavior. One foolish moment on the pornography playground can demolish it all.

My friend Don was a respected pastor of a megachurch in a nearby city. He was married with children and grandchildren. He enjoyed a stellar reputation as a denominational leader, solid preacher, and gifted administrator. One day he was caught looking at pornography on his church computer. This led to more revelations of a long-standing pornography habit. What he spent decades building came crashing down overnight. Today he is out of ministry and trying to make a living in a new career as he picks up the pieces of his shattered life.

> We spend our lives inflating the balloon of respect. It only takes one pin to pop it.

Let's apply this powerful dose of preventive medicine. How many times does a man's wife need to catch him viewing pornography before it strikes a mortal wound to his marriage? How will he measure the damage if one of his children catches him playing with himself in front of a computer screen? How many porno cookies on your work computer will need to accumulate before your job and livelihood are in serious jeopardy?

I am not trying to scare you to death. Actually, I am trying to scare you to life. After all, the Bible does say, "Do not be deceived: God cannot be mocked. A man reaps what he sows. The one who sows to please his sinful nature, from that nature will reap destruction" (Gal. 6:7, 8). We cannot forget the warning that our sins will find us out (Num. 32:23).

Too many people think they will beat the odds only to discover that reputation and testimony are very fragile in the face of persistent sin and risky behavior. We spend our lives inflating the balloon of respect. It only takes one pin to pop it.

In the battle for our integrity and testimony, we need to make wise decisions that will serve as building blocks for a lasting reputation and fulfilled life. Proverbs 13:21 puts it in perspective when it promises, "Trouble chases sinners, while blessings chase the righteous!"

Excavation began for the World Trade Center in 1966. By 1971, tenants began to move in on the ground floors even as the upper floors were still being constructed. The formal dedication of the Twin Towers was delayed until 1973. The south tower (WTC 2), which had been struck second by the 9/11 terrorists, was the first to suffer a complete structural collapse at 10:05 a.m., 62 minutes after being hit. The north tower (WTC 1) collapsed at 10:29 a.m., 104 minutes following the impact of the airliner. In spite of millions of dollars of invested capital and years of state-of-the-art construction, these icons of free enterprise and crown jewels of the New York skyline were gone. Their collapse took less than two hours.

Remember, porn-terror threatens your integrity daily. Keep those lust-piloted planes grounded through a firm resolve to preserve your hard-earned reputation.

---

## Positive Truth
## Reason #15

I can guard against pornography's destructive attacks
on the integrity of my Christian testimony by
acknowledging my vulnerabilities and
maintaining a strong, constant defense.

## 16

# I promote health and harmony in the body of Christ.

**WE ALL HAVE** been touched in some way by the dreaded devastation of cancer. My father is a cancer survivor. My mother was a cancer victim. I am sure your family can relate. In 2002, cancer accounted for almost 25 percent of deaths in the United States.[39]

Cancer is a disease that starts in our cells. Our bodies are made up of millions of cells, grouped together to form organs or tissues such as the lungs, liver, muscles, and bones. Genes inside each cell order it to grow, work, reproduce, and die.

Normally, these orders are clear. Our cells obey, and we remain healthy. Sometimes a cell's instructions get mixed up and it behaves abnormally. After a while, groups of abnormal cells form lumps or tumors.

Tumors can be either benign (noncancerous) or malignant (cancerous). Benign tumor cells stay in one place in the body and are not usually life-threatening.

Malignant tumor cells are able to invade the tissues around them and spread to other parts of the body. Cancerous cells that spread to other parts of the body are called metastases. The first sign that a malignant tumor has spread often is swelling of nearby lymph nodes, but cancer can metastasize to almost any part of the body. Malignant tumors can be dangerous. It is important to find them and treat them quickly before they spread.

Our Creator has very deliberately chosen to describe the life and relationships of his people as a *body*. The descriptions are very specific in comparing our function together as Christians as analogous to the dynamics of a physical body. This "body of Christ" is composed of many parts. The Bible is very clear about our interdependence as members of His church. There is no such thing as an independent cell.

The apostle Paul wrote in Galatians 5:9, "But it takes only one wrong person among you to infect all the others—a little yeast spreads quickly through the whole batch of dough!" (NLT).

As believers, we are called and empowered to obey the orders of the Lord. But when we get confused and out of step with His will, spiritual cancer occurs, eventually forming a malignant tumor.

When I sin, my spiritual health is affected. Soon others are infected with my virus of spiritual apathy, deception, and dullness. Whether I see it or not, whether I agree with it or not, it is the truth.

> Avoiding the grip of pornography is an act of loving service to the rest of the body of Christ.

Brad was a youth pastor with a well-concealed pornography problem. Over time, this led him to the typical existence in the gray twilight between fantasy and reality. Even though he had a beautiful, dedicated wife and three small children, the porn images cultivated an attraction toward some of the teenage girls.

Over time, people began to observe him in inappropriate private settings with girls. Eventually, reports of romantic conversations began to surface. One day, he left a note for his wife stating that he was leaving the family. She began to do some

THINK BEFORE YOU LOOK

research and found love letters to girls in the youth department and evidence of extensive amounts of pornography in their computer.

Not only did he devastate his family, but also the entire youth department erupted in turmoil. The fallout affected the entire congregation.

As I write this chapter, Brad and his wife are at a counseling clinic seeking help. Sadly, Brad is not responding to this spiritual radiation treatment. The cancer of uncontrolled lust has him blinded to his sin. He now seems unable to deal with reality. We are praying for a healing of his soul, his family, the youth department, and the congregation. But the malignant tumor has definitely done some major damage.

In the face of temptation, I must affirm the fact that purity promotes spiritual health for me, my family, and my network of Christian friends. Avoiding the grip of pornography is an act of loving service to the rest of the body of Christ.

## Positive Truth
## Reason #16

When I avoid pornography I promote health and harmony in the body of Christ, serving as a positive and pure contributor to others.

# 17

# I cultivate a stronger resistance to future interpersonal sexual sin.

T HOMAS JEFFERSON warned, "Do not bite at the bait of pleasure till you know there is no hook beneath it." Sadly, when it comes to pornography, there is always a hook of some kind. Once we are snagged, we are led away to destructive patterns of living.

As I am writing these chapters, another sad news story about the tragic effect of porn has hit the headlines. In Lodi, California, a fourteen-year-old girl ran away. A forty-two-year-old local fire captain spearheaded the effort to find her. Two weeks after her disappearance, the girl surfaced by making contact with her therapist. The community was shocked to learn that the fire captain had been arrested on suspicion of forcible rape, committing lewd acts upon a child, and sexual battery. The runaway offered her therapist accounts of the fire captain sexually assaulting her over a span of several months. As is always the case, authorities suspected a porn problem and seized his home computer. They found graphic preteen child porn and also charged him with three counts of possession of child pornography.

I would suspect that years ago when the fire captain first started looking at porn, he never expected it would lead to jail time. But this is the nature of all sin, and porn in particular. By rehearsing sexual scenes in your mind over and over again, you pave the way for eventually acting out these passions and perversions.

Virtually all child molesters have a porn problem. Virtually all rapists have a porn problem. Stalkers have a porn problem. Voyeurs have a porn problem. Most adulterers struggle with pornography. Many young people engaged in premarital sexual escapades have been stimulated and coached to this behavior by viewing porn.

Pornography erodes our integrity, social awareness, spiritual resolve, and moral constraint. Of course, not everyone who glances at an erotic Web page is going to go out and rape someone next week. However, every pornographic episode is a mental rehearsal for eventual acts that could destroy your life.

> "There is no man that lives that can't be broken down, provided it is the right temptation, put in the right spot."

Think of erosion. Entire shorelines are lost and houses fall off seaside cliffs because each day as the waves roll in, they carry away just a handful of sand. One drop of water on its own isn't enough to destroy a rock, but repeated drops in the same place for years will eventually change the shape of the rock, even destroy it.

I remember seeing a picture of Flower Pot Island in Tobermory, Ontario. Formations in the shape of flower pots have been created through years of water lapping against the rock. These formerly massive and solid pieces of shoreline rock have become odd-looking, top-heavy, fragile structures because of years of erosion.

So it is with our lives. No one is impervious to the erosion of eroticism. Engaging in consistent episodes of the mind through porn paves the way for behaviors previously unimagined.

Henry Ward Beecher warned, "All men are tempted. There is no man that lives that can't be broken down, provided it is the right temptation, put in the right spot."[40] Small cracks can ruin the foundation of a home, the value of a collectable, or the usefulness of a glass. In time a small crack of unchecked lust can lead to a collapse of true love and reason.

C. S. Lewis observed:

Only those who try to resist temptation know how strong it is. A man who gives into temptation after five minutes simply does not know what it would have been like an hour later. That is why bad people, in one sense, know very little about badness. They have lived a sheltered life by always giving in.[41]

No one wants to land in the headlines under arrest for some bizarre sexual behavior. Those who have found themselves there never planned to get there either. But it happens. Porn paves the way, ignites the passions, and dulls the senses.

I've heard it said that every moment of resistance to temptation is a victory. These small victories every day, every week, are the stuff of a noble and pure life.

---

## Positive Truth
## Reason #17

As I avoid pornography, I cultivate a stronger resistance to future interpersonal sexual sin and its many destructive consequences.

---

# 18

# I nurture the proper biblical view of the sanctity of womanhood.

**P**ERHAPS THE MOST important philosophical and moral battle raging in our culture today concerns the value of human life. Pro-life groups work to protect the unborn baby because they believe all life is sacred. Other groups battle euthanasia because the elderly are intrinsically valuable, not because of their vigor or usefulness to society, but because they are created in the image of God. Thousands of charitable organizations work to relieve poverty, provide for the homeless, and feed the starving because all humans should live in dignity with the basic provisions of life.

Abortionists, suicide doctors, euthanasia proponents, and ruthless dictators all have one thing in common: they do not value human life. Pornography moguls are also members of this notorious club. They demean the sanctity and dignity of women.

A holy respect for women has its roots in the story of biblical creation. The scriptural narrative begins with God's majesty, bringing the world into existence through His creative word. After the first five days of creation, He looked at His magnificent world and declared it to be "good." On the sixth day He created Adam in His own image and declared him "very good."

But Adam was alone, and this was "not good" (Gen. 2:18). God knew there was something extremely important missing. After finishing the naming of all the animals, Adam probably began to realize he had no counterpart. As his aloneness became obvious, God revealed His sacred plan. Woman would be the crowning touch in the picture of creation—and would complete man's existence.

Unlike Adam, she was not created from the dust. Instead, she was taken from Adam's side, thus demonstrating the interdependence that would exist between man and woman. She would meet Adam's needs in a way that even the Creator could not. The Divine Master Artist spared none of His beauty and wonder when He created the female.

As Adam woke from the operating table and soon discovered his counterpart, we can only imagine the delight, affection, appreciation, and honor that must have filled his soul. "They were naked and felt no shame" (Gen. 2:25). This scene of intimacy and respect, prior to the spiritual fall of humanity, is a picture we must always remember in order to value the sanctity and dignity of women in today's world.

> Women do two-thirds of the world's work, grow at least 50 percent of the world's food, and still have time to produce every single one of the world's babies.

As history unfolds and mankind struggles with sin, God reiterates the honor, beauty, and sanctity of women. A very brief summary reminds us that:

◆ a woman's value is far beyond precious stones as she is unusually skilled at bringing dignity, blessing, and well-being to the lives of family members. As a result she is to be praised (Prov. 31:10–31).

- a noble woman is her husband's joy and crown (Prov. 12:4).
- we are to exhibit a spirit of submission to women, honoring their needs and wishes above our own (Eph. 5:21).
- women are to be loved and cherished even as Christ loves, cherishes, and provides for His people (Eph. 5:22–33).

Author Charles Swindoll offers this perspective.

The Bible is full of great women. So is history. Along with the Joan of Arcs and the Florence Nightingales and the Madame Curies and the Mother Teresas we find countless other nameless mothers, sisters, and daughters. Abraham Lincoln said, "No man is poor who has had a godly mother." He, like many great and accomplished people fiercely linked his success to his mother. Military heroes, political statesmen, ministers of the Gospel, athletes, media personalities, literary and musical geniuses alike have attributed the development and cultivation of their skills to their mothers and/or their wives. Down through the history of time marches an endless succession of courageous and visionary women, virtuous women, self-sacrificing women.[42]

From a practical standpoint, it is good to remember that women do two-thirds of the world's work, grow at least 50 percent of the world's food, and still have time to produce every single one of the world's babies.[43]

The pornography industry creates a vision of women that is completely opposed to this wholesome perspective. They become objects to be used and abused, tossed in bed, then tossed aside. They are depicted in unbelievably dishonoring and despicable ways, often being manipulated and used by multiple men.

Would you want your mother being pictured in these ways? How about your sister? How would you feel about your daughter being sexually violated by three or four porn-star perverts? If you are married, how about your wife? If you are single, how about your future wife?

Every female porn star is someone's daughter or sister. Some are even mothers. Most importantly, they were made in the image of God and they are daughters of Eve, beloved by the heavenly Father. They were designed for dignity, not sexual disdain. They were created as sacred, not as sex objects. Even though they may not respect themselves enough to say "no" to the porn promoters, you and I can respect them enough to ignore their shameful exploits. We have no God-given right to violate the sacredness and dignity of a woman by looking on her nakedness.

To be against abortion, euthanasia, starvation, and other plights that degrade human dignity but to support and view pornography is a contradiction in the worst fashion.

We honor womanhood when we avoid porn. Every mother, sister, and daughter is worthy of this respect, even if the porn industry has trampled them underfoot in a money-motivated determination to use and abuse the women of any and every society.

## Positive Truth
## Reason #18

By resisting pornography, I nurture the proper biblical view of the sanctity of womanhood and show honor toward all the women in my life.

# 19

# I relate to women as equals and persons of ultimate worth.

**THE TWISTED** and disrespectful view of women described in the previous chapter has resulted in a tragic breakdown of relationship skills between the sexes.

College campuses are increasingly unsafe for women in our society. Rape is rampant. Perverts stalk and spy on women. Sexual predators seem to be multiplying. Orgies almost seem like the norm in the dorm. Sexually transmitted diseases have become so commonplace they are even advertising treatments on national television these days. Out-of-wedlock pregnancies are common. Of course, most pregnancies are averted through the free distribution of condoms and contraceptives as the "girls gone wild" culture dominates many segments of college life in America. For many reasons, it is a serious problem in our society.

As a side note, all school campuses seem to be dangerous these days. A U.S. Department of Education report released in June 2003 contends that, at some point, almost 10 percent of all students are victims of sexual misconduct—ranging from lewd comments to rape—by school staff.[44]

Fueling the frenzy, many colleges regularly embrace pornography in classrooms and campus events in the name of academic freedom, intellectual inquiry, and free speech. Professors and administrators cannot seem to understand how the prevalence of porn is affecting behavior between young men and women, compounding the moral unraveling of society.

Researcher Mary Anne Layden, director of the Center for Cognitive Therapy at the University of Pennsylvania, has conducted some amazing studies demonstrating how porn affects the brain and the behavior, especially of men toward women.

Through a study originally geared toward the brain function of cocaine addicts, evidence has demonstrated some disturbing activity in the brains of normal people exposed to pornography. Researchers put together a test group of cocaine addicts and a control group of people with no known addictions or personality disorders, then took PET scans of their brains while they viewed pictures of animals, and another set while they looked at pictures of other people taking cocaine. The cocaine addicts' brains had a dramatically different response to the photos of people using drugs than to the animal photos. Non-addicts' brains showed no significant differences.

But when researchers showed the control group pornographic photos, different areas of their brains lit up and their PET scans closely resembled those of the cocaine addicts while they were looking at the photos of drug use.

Layden observes:

That sets up some interesting questions. We're seeing the same symptoms in porn addicts as we do in cocaine addicts—but it's harder for the porn addict to go into remission than the cocaine addict, and they're more likely to relapse. When you're treating cocaine addicts, you start with detox to get it out of their system before you start counseling. But with a porn addict, that substance can be called up at a moment's notice, forever.

Any lesson learned in the presence of arousal will be learned better, remembered longer and acted on more often.

She goes on to note that with porn, we are dealing with a permanently implanted addictive substance. So, it's a very hard disorder to treat.

Then Layden offers a very disturbing commentary:

The problem with pornography isn't just in the way the images adhere themselves to a person's memory. It's in the messages they send. Sexual violence perpetrators have permission-giving beliefs. There's the rape myth, that women like it, need it, etc. There are similar pedophile myths. All are permission-giving beliefs, and all are transmitted in pornography.

Commenting on the promotion of porn on college campuses she notes, "They (porn images) are damaging to normal relationships and encouraging to pathology and violence, so I can't imagine why we would want to show them to young people. There are classes on campus that talk about LSD, but you won't get any of it."[45]

Pornography has been called the "true hate literature" of our age, because of its dehumanization and exploitation of the person, regardless of size, shape, color, or gender. Evaluating how pornography has affected the way that men in our culture view and treat women, Laurie Hall wrote,

Believing that others are here for our use and enjoyment, we discard them when the momentary pleasure is over. We say whatever it takes to get what we want. We absolutely do not feel we have any responsibility to those we have used. Having eaten, we wipe our mouths and move on, searching for someone else to devour. Our paths are littered with pregnant girlfriends, rejected wives, and abandoned children.[46]

Stay with me here. I want to enhance this very important point with just a few more insights, and then make an application. In his book, *Wild at Heart,* John Eldredge expands on this issue with added insight:

Most men want the maiden without any sort of cost to themselves. They want all the joys of the beauty without any of the woes of the battle. This is the sinister nature of pornography— enjoying the woman at her expense. Pornography is what happens when a man insists on being energized by a woman; he uses her to get a feeling that he is a man. It is a false strength, as I've said, because it depends on an outside source rather than emanating from deep within his center. And it is the paragon of selfishness.[47]

> Pornography has been called the "true hate literature" of our age, because of its dehumanization and exploitation of the person, regardless of size, shape, color, or gender.

I know you are thinking: "I've never raped a woman. I don't disrespect the women in my circle of acquaintances. I don't take advantage of ladies." Perhaps this is true. But this does not negate the facts about porn and the general, documented reality that porn will, in time, impact the way you view and treat women.

Our goal is to stay on a path of mental habits, heart commitments, truly caring conversation, and honorable behavior that treats women with ultimate respect and genuine care. Staying away from pornography may just be the best thing you can do to achieve this important goal.

In his landmark book *Every Man's Battle*, coauthor Fred Stoeker gives us a valuable perspective.

> Jesus' hands never touched a woman with dishonor, but Jesus said that lusting with the eyes is the same as touching. Given that Jesus was sinless, I suddenly realized that Jesus not only never touched a woman with dishonor, He never even looked at a woman in dishonor. Could I say that?

Then in response to the objection of some that he is being a bit too hard on himself and that it is natural to look at women lustfully, Stoeker adds,

> What you're doing is stealing. That impure thought life is the life of a thief. You're stealing images that aren't yours. When you had premarital sex, you touched someone who didn't belong to you. When you looked down the blouse of a woman who wasn't your wife, you were stealing something that isn't yours to take. . . . When we're thieves with our eyes, we're embezzling sexual gratification from areas that don't belong to us, from women who aren't connected to us.[48]

In these last two chapters, we (hopefully) have recommitted our hearts to a biblical view of the dignity and sanctity of women. While noting that porn undermines this view, we also realize that we will ultimately live out our image of women in how we interact and relate to them. Let's start a movement of purity and honor as we walk away from the damaging influence of pornography and renew our minds with the holy and honorable perspectives of biblical truth.

## Positive Truth
## Reason #19

By avoiding the superficial and self-serving world of porn, I am able to consistently relate to women as equals and persons of ultimate worth.

# 20

# I learn to live in reality rather than fantasy.

**MARY KAY LETOURNEAU** was described in a recent news story as having had a sterling record of accomplishment while in prison. During her seven years in the Washington State Corrections Center for Women, the former teacher tutored inmates, bolstered the prison textbook collection, sang in the choir, and rarely missed mass.

In response to this account of her "sterling" behavior, one of Letourneau's best friends could only say, "The facets to this woman are unfathomable." You see, Letourneau is the famed schoolteacher who carried on an obsessive affair with one of her students, Vili Fualaau. As *People* magazine describes it, "She was a Republican congressman's daughter and a mother of four with a crumbling marriage. He was a talented artist from a broken home. She was thirty-four. He was twelve. Americans were shocked—and perversely transfixed." The affair produced two daughters.

Most of society wonders how a person can behave as Letourneau did. To some who know her well, Letourneau is simply stuck in her own private neverland. "Mary has this remarkable ability to block out reality and rationalize her actions—she lives in a fantasy world," says Michelle Jarvis, an estranged friend. Fualaau's mother reiterated this observation in a court statement when she complained that the perverted teacher "lives in a fantasy world and she has engulfed my son in this fantasy world."[49]

Letourneau was not born into a fantasy world. She got there one step at a time through choices and actions that began to cloud and eventually take over reality. When the fantasies are sex-related, they are particularly powerful and deceiving.

Of course, fantasy is not always a bad thing. Children's books, family-oriented amusement parks, novels, and movies invite normal people into a fantasy world that provides wholesome entertainment and life lessons that can enrich our journey. But a fantasy land is a place you only want to visit; it is not a good place to stay for very long. And, we need to be very selective about who produces the fantasy and why. Some fantasy visits can destroy the realities of life.

> Reality, not fantasy, provides countless opportunities to love and be loved. Eternity rewards those who live, love, and serve—in reality.

My wife loves to read good, wholesome fiction. She finds it captivating and entertaining. I, on the other hand, pride myself in reading only nonfiction. I guess I do not have time to read for entertainment, only for learning and skill development. In reality, it is quite a driven and boring approach.

But there is a very scary fantasy land most men have visited too often. The invitation comes through steamy magazines (even the ones sitting at the grocery store checkout), Web pages, and daydreams stimulated by the sight of an attractive woman. It appears at first to be a wonderful destination, but experience tells us all we do not want to go through those gates and certainly do not want to stay there.

Just as a matter of perspective, let's consider how the pornographic fantasy world works. It appears so inviting at the front door, but as soon as you enter and stay awhile, things take a dramatic and often destructive turn for the worse.

Dr. Victor Cline, a psychotherapist who has treated hundreds of pornography addicts, has clarified the corridors of this fantasy world. Dr. Cline identifies addiction as the first trap in the world of lust and porn. The pleasure keeps a person coming back for regular visits. This leads to escalation. The initial fantasies no longer excite. More explicit, deviant, and even violent images become the norm. Desensitization occurs next in the journey into the fantasy world. What was once repulsive now seems normal, even to the point of assuming that everyone must be doing these things. The fourth and darkest step of the journey involves "acting out" through risky and destructive behaviors like voyeurism, exhibitionism, adultery, rape, molestation, even murder.[50]

Another description of the journey into sexual fantasy land has been described as the Centerfold Syndrome by Gary R. Brooks, assistant chief of psychology at the Veterans Administration Center in Temple, Texas. The earliest symptom of an overstay in the fantasy zone is *voyeurism*, which involves a preference to looking at women rather then interacting with them. Next is *objectification* where women become objects based on how their bodies offer sexual satisfaction. *Validation* is the next step into the dark world. This involves a sense of validation based on a connection with sexy women with no concern for their character. *Trophyism* is the attitude of viewing women as trophies to be displayed as personal property or subjects of a conquest. The final and sad stop for this Centerfold Syndrome is a fear of and *inability for true intimacy* in which a man can no longer relate to women at a spiritual or emotional level but only as sexual objects.[51]

The point of these more clinical summaries is to give you a thumbnail sketch of sexual fantasy land, and the progressive allure and resulting damage. It is not a place you want to frequent.

As I write this book, I have just reviewed Dr. James Dobson's interview with serial killer Ted Bundy. It is a powerful reminder of the ultimate trap of a fantasy world. In the interview, Bundy stated every man he met in the prison system who was motivated to commit violence was deeply involved in and addicted to pornography. Bundy agreed with FBI studies that the most common interest serial killers have is pornography. He even declared his fear for society based on the graphic sex-related violence that is so common in today's media and is being piped right into the average home. Destructive sexual fantasy is being shoved down our throats daily.

Reality beats this fantasy hands down. Reality is filled with day-to-day intimacy with God and others. Reality is incredibly exhilarating as you tune into the extraordinary beauty of life. Reality calls you to find true fulfillment by serving others rather than being consumed with your own passions and confused needs. Reality reminds us of the joys of purity and holiness every day. Reality provides countless opportunities to love and be loved. Eternity rewards those who live, love, and serve—in reality.

This is another powerful reason to stay far away from the flashing welcome signs to the world of sexual fantasy.

## Positive Truth
## Reason #20

I embrace the rewarding world of reality rather than floundering in the emptiness of fantasy when I prevail over pornography.

# 21

# I steer clear of unnecessary personal guilt and shame.

**G**UILT HAS BEEN described as the gift that keeps on giving. Writer Samuel Johnson observed, "Guilt once harbored in the conscious breast, intimidates the brave, degrades the great." It was Shakespeare who noted, "Suspicion always haunts the guilty mind."

In a previous chapter, we spoke of the positive benefit of keeping a soft and sensitive conscience. This is maintained through regular confession of sin before God and the commitment to keep short accounts with others.

Porn promotes a unique kind of guilt and shame that takes on a life of its own. Not only does its chronic presence undermine a clear conscience, it also dramatically changes a man for the worse.

Paul talks about two types of guilt in his second letter to the Corinthians. After issuing a call to repentance, he knew that his words brought pain and conviction. However, the fruit of their response demonstrated a godly type of sorrow—a genuine change.

But in this passage, he writes about another kind of response. It involves sorrow, harm, regret, even death. This is called "worldly" sorrow, and I believe it speaks of guilt that goes unresolved over time. Read Paul's words for yourself.

Even if I caused you sorrow by my letter, I do not regret it. Though I did regret it—I see that my letter hurt you, but only for a little while—yet now I am happy, not because you were made sorry, but because your sorrow led you to repentance. For you became sorrowful as God intended and so were not harmed in any way by us. Godly sorrow brings repentance that leads to salvation and leaves no regret, but worldly sorrow brings death. See what this godly sorrow has produced in you: what earnestness, what eagerness to clear yourselves, what indignation, what alarm, what longing, what concern, what readiness to see justice done. At every point you have proved yourselves to be innocent in this matter (2 Cor. 7:8–11).

An obsession with sex, porn, and masturbation wears down a man's sense of dignity. Even though he resolves to stop, he returns over and over again. He confesses his failure to God but even in his heart doubts his sincerity, knowing he will repeat his actions. He loses confidence and begins to withdraw from spiritual leadership in the home and the church.

> Guilt and shame are the devil's tools to condemn us into believing that we are bad and beyond God's forgiveness.

In fact, the guilty man will often withdraw from a variety of activities and relationships due to strong feelings of guilt. Just as Adam and Eve hid themselves from the Lord after their sin (Gen. 3:13), so men with reoccurring, unresolved sexual obsession will hide and retreat.

Author Jeff Olson writes:

Certainly men should feel bad after they've looked at porn, but not in the way they normally do. The sorrow they usually feel is not a productive godly sorrow. It doesn't lead them to a greater sense of forgiveness and a growing desire to serve God and others (2 Cor. 7:10). The sorrow men typically feel is a worldly sorrow that drives them further from meaningful relationships and endeavors and deeper into a self-absorbed, safer way of life.[52]

Shame is the natural bedfellow for this kind of guilt. Guilt is a sense of condemnation because of one's actions. Shame is a feeling of worthlessness because of unresolved guilt. It is the devil's tool to condemn us into believing that we are bad and beyond God's forgiveness. Olson adds:

Men who use pornography find self-imposed shame easier to live with than the risk of rejection by others. They instinctively know that the path of real honor and dignity leads to the risks of honest relationships. Although deep inside they want to open up and be more involved with others, they feel inadequate or fearful that others won't be able to accept them as they are.[53]

This guilt and shame cycle is part of what is so devastating about the choice to engage with porn. So, what is the solution?

As we've already noted, every man must fully embrace the truth that sets the soul free. We must subject the overwhelming feelings of guilt and shame to objective realities that spring from God's word. Focus on these truths:

- ◆ God loves me, no matter what I do or do not do. His love for me is not based on my performance but on His person (character of love).
- ◆ Christ died to set me free from guilt and shame.

- Because of His grace, I am a new creation—perfectly loved, fully accepted, and totally empowered.
- This behavior is inconsistent with my relationship to the Lord and violates my core identity.
- I do not have to live like this and can be absolutely free from this bondage.
- I will consistently and genuinely confess any actions that break my fellowship with the Lord, asking for a spirit of genuine repentance.
- To demonstrate that repentance, I must take bold steps with the true desire to change.
- I will pursue authentic relationships with the Lord and others.
- I will ask for help from trusted friends, counselors, or pastors.
- I will persevere in the direction of freedom, realizing it will take time but keeping my vision clear toward victory.

Unloading the burden of guilt and shame is liberating and essential to spiritual vitality. Even though you may occasionally pick it back up, treat it like a hot potato and put it back on the cross where it belongs. That's a feeling worth cherishing as you avoid porn and experience increasing success.

---

### Positive Truth
### Reason #21

By steering clear of the unnecessary personal guilt and shame of pornography, I will enjoy a wholesome and holy experience of life as God meant it to be.

## 22

# I cultivate a lifestyle of contentment and satisfaction.

**I**N THE FAMOUS rock ballad, Mick Jagger and the Rolling Stones proclaimed, "I can't get no satisfaction."

We may not live Jagger's life or sing his song, but we certainly understand his problem. Discontent is one of the great diseases of the day.

Our inability to find satisfaction is partly due to advertising, which is primarily designed to cultivate and promote discontent. Images of new products make the things you own appear out of style and out of step with the times. Think about it. A hundred years ago, Farmer Fred had no idea his overalls were not adequate because there was no television marketer telling him he was dressed like a nerd compared with other people.

Porn is the most dangerous promoter of discontent in our society. The dissatisfaction cultivated by the airbrushed images and the ever-willing "lovers" will cost more than a new closet of clothes or this year's latest car. Porn-promoted dissatisfaction will cost you your very well-being. We've already noted the relational ineptitude incited by pornography. It can eat up precious time, money, imagination, and energy. Dissatisfaction is guaranteed.

Discontent is essentially an attitude that questions the goodness, faithfulness, and provision of God in your life. Counselors and researchers agree that a fixation with porn and masturbation is usually a misguided attempt to escape pain, compensate for disappointment, or avoid difficult circumstances.

Contentment learns to cope with pain, accept disappointment, and face difficult circumstances in light of the sufficiency and goodness of God.

The words typically utilized to communicate the idea of contentment in our English Bibles actually mean "sufficiency" and encourage a spirit

> Porn is the most dangerous promoter of discontent in our society.

of having "all we need." As Jerry Bridges has written, "The contented person experiences the sufficiency of God's provision for his needs and the sufficiency of God's grace for his circumstances." He adds, "The godly person has found what the greedy or envious or discontented person always searches for but never finds. He has found satisfaction and rest in his soul."[54] Yes, godliness with contentment is great gain.

Unfortunately, instead of fixing our eyes on the Lord, we fixate on the things around us. Comparison is an ugly game because there are always winners and losers. We are usually the losers.

By comparing and complaining, we have taken our eyes off the goodness and sufficiency of God. In fact, we question His goodness for not giving us the problem-free life of another or for not blessing us with the things someone else may have.

Bridges has also observed that the very first temptation in the history of mankind was the temptation to be discontent. Adam and Eve had abundance in the garden but chose to question the sufficiency of God's provision and the goodness of His plan. It may not be your first temptation, but it is one of the most common. The belief that the grass is always greener on the other side of the fence is one of the most commonly used proverbs in our world of discontent, envy, and jealousy.

Interestingly enough, one scientist has actually corroborated this idea. James Pomerantz, in a scientific article on " 'The Grass Is Always Greener': An Ecological Analysis of an Old Aphorism" (1983), found that optical and perceptual laws alone will make the grass at a distance look greener to the human eye than the blades of grass perpendicular to the ground.[55]

Of course, we've all seen a cow or a horse trying to get at that preferred patch of grass just on the other side of the fence. And since people are equally dissatisfied with their lot in life, it should not surprise anyone that a modern psychologist has spoken of "the 'greener grass' phenomenon" by which modern individuals continually evaluate supposedly better alternatives for themselves.

If we removed the fences and just looked at the open pasture we would find that the grass is greener where it is most watered. The comparisons we make based on where the "fences" are positioned can be very deceiving. Obviously, we need to evaluate wisely and water regularly the grass of our own life.

Pornography is the act of watering the wrong grass. It leads us away from the regular commitment to water the vital life-giving resources of our walk with God, our relationships with others and the goodness of the life God has allotted us.

A Chinese proverb reminds us, "There is no calamity greater than lavish desires, no greater guilt than discontentment and no greater disaster than greed."

We need to stop looking around comparing ourselves with others and complaining about how bad our life is. Instead, we can trust God for the grace to look to Him with gratitude for His goodness, sufficiency, and providence in our lives.

As we do so, our hearts change. We will not look for quick escapes to cope with life. We can be content with God's sufficiency and goodness in our circumstance, problems and all.

We can also be content with who we are. Neil Clark Warren has written:

> The secret of contentment lies in discovering who in the world you are—and mobilizing your courage to be that person. The richest and deepest contentment is a natural result of achieving authenticity—that is, knowing yourself intimately, appreciating your unique gifts and abilities, and making choices moment by moment that demonstrate honor and respect for yourself.[56]

You can achieve contentment by resting in the goodness and grace of God. He is your faithful and perfect provider. He is sovereign over your life. He loves you and is working through your pain and problems to make you more like Him. He values you in Christ, so there is no need to compare yourself with anyone else. You can live content, pure, and free. That's your destiny in Him.

We do not need to fuel our discontent through an escape to pornland. Contentment and gratitude are good for you, much better than a self-focused reaction to the challenges of life.

## Positive Truth
## Reason #22

By resisting pornography and resting in the goodness
and grace of God, I will cultivate a lifestyle of
contentment and satisfaction.

# 23

# I experience the blessing of living as a servant.

**O**NE OF THE most profound statements in the Gospels is Jesus's declaration to His self-seeking disciples that "the Son of Man did not come to be served, but to serve, and to give His life a ransom for many" (Matt. 20:28). In another context, He declared, "But I am among you as the one who serves" (Luke 22:27). Paul described our Lord by saying that He "made himself nothing, taking the very nature of a servant, being made in human likeness. And being found in appearance as a man, he humbled himself and became obedient to death—even death on a cross!" (Phil. 2:7, 8).

The prophet Isaiah described the coming Messiah as a suffering, self-giving servant (Isa. 52:13—53:12). Yet Jesus disclosed the pleasure and power of servanthood when He said, "It is more blessed to give than to receive" (Acts 20:35).

Contrast our Lord's example with the confession of a young man named Randy who went to counseling for his obsessive masturbation. He wrote, "Masturbation physically is a self-bent thing. Its focus is inward. It doesn't share. It doesn't know the verb 'to give.' It is a fire that feeds itself."

C. S. Lewis agreed:

For me the real evil of masturbation would be that it takes an appetite which in lawful use, leads the individual out of himself to complete his own personality in that of another and turns it back; sends the man back into the prison of himself, there to keep a harem of imaginary brides.[57]

No doubt one of the most tragic ramifications of a captivation with pornography and masturbation is the way in which it undermines true servanthood. It is ultimately a self-serving approach to sexuality. It is a self-absorbed habit. It is a self-adoring action. As Lewis observed, it is "the prison of self."

In ways that he may not even perceive, the habitual pornographer can create a universe in which he becomes the center. The need for release, the calculating of repeated fantasies and moments of private pleasure, and the self-focused drain of energy can overtake his life. The implications are many.

To truly walk in the steps of Jesus is to trust Him for His supernatural grace, "not to be served." It is to embrace His heart each day by spending your energies on others through humble sacrifice. This path leads to increased happiness because Jesus promoted by His example and promised in His teachings that by giving, we truly receive.

> In ways that he may not even perceive, the habitual pornographer can create a universe in which he becomes the center.

What a powerful image to remember. Jesus, while facing all the temptations common to mankind, never acted in a selfish way. If you are a true believer, He lives in you to demonstrate that same character to a needy world. Channel your energies to others and discover the path of real happiness.

## Positive Truth
## Reason #23

I will experience the Christ-honoring blessing of living as a servant by overcoming the self-indulgent and self-worshiping habits of pornography.

# 24

# I learn the relational skills of authentic intimacy.

**N A RECENT** survey of a very large congregation in North America, the question was asked, "What do you fear the most?" The primary answer from the pew was a bit startling: "intimacy with God."

Many of us suffer from relational AIDS (Acute Intimacy Deficiency Syndrome). It is difficult to be truly close and vulnerable with God or with people.

To clarify, when I speak of intimacy I speak of a "no holds barred" relationship of open communication, a heart-to-heart connection, and a deep sense of mutual belonging. My friend Steve Korch says it so clearly when he writes,

> Intimacy is authentic closeness in a personal relationship. It is about what happens between two individuals who genuinely draw near to one another. It includes sensations of joyful confidence, gracious understanding, relaxed presence, perpetual attraction, and warm affection. With intimacy, there is a heightened sense of respect that removes the stiff formality that stretches the seams between two people who are unsure of each other. It is both moving toward another and likewise allowing that person the freedom to approach. It brings the delightful

experience of sharing personal space in the midst of a very private and alienated world.[58]

In the book *Every Woman's Desire: Every Man's Guide to Winning the Heart of a Woman,* the authors reveal these facts:

- 84 percent of women feel they don't have intimacy (oneness) in their marriages.
- 83 percent of women feel their husbands don't even know the basic needs of a woman for intimacy (oneness) or how to provide intimacy for them.
- A large majority of female divorcées say that their married years were the loneliest years of their lives.[59]

Pornography is the tool of choice for most men in avoiding the demands and disappointments of real intimacy. As Harry Schaumburg notes in his landmark work *False Intimacy,* "A sex addict creates pseudo-relationships with something or someone who can be controlled, such as a picture, an actor on the video screen, or a prostitute in order to avoid relational pain."[60] Whether the relational pain involves the frustration of not being able to find intimacy as an unmarried person or the fear of becoming too intimate with a spouse, the results are equally damaging.

> Many of us suffer from relational AIDS (Acute Intimacy Deficiency Syndrome).

Intimacy is threatening, especially to men, and for a variety of reasons. For many of us, intimacy is unfamiliar. We grew up with an absent or angry dad. Perhaps our mother was controlling. Maybe our family of origin is filled with conflict and dysfunction. The confusion and pain promote withdrawal. In a world of machismo, we learn not to talk about feelings. We bury our vulnerabilities and begin a (sometimes) lifelong pattern of emotional isolation.

It is hard work to unlearn the negative lessons from growing up. Even if you had a normal and loving home, the reality of being vulnerable, communicative, forgiving, and understanding is very demanding.

Millions are trying to find intimacy online.

> In separate studies, researchers found people who spent more than thirty hours a week online were divorced from spouses and fired from jobs as a result of distractions. They are considering an official classification of this tendency as a specific disorder.[61]

Psychologist David Greenfield discovered in a recent survey of over eighteen thousand people that most people go online to find *intimacy*. Unfortunately, their idea of intimacy is cheap, quick sex or a largely artificial relationship with others through newsgroups or chat rooms. In response to this research, one counselor offers this keen observation:

> That kind of interaction also allows individuals the opportunity to hide all of their weaknesses while exaggerating their strengths. It's easy for people to feel close with someone who is always able to "put their best foot forward." We all want to be able to grow close to someone else while being able to also cover up bad things. Regrettably, all close relationships eventually have to address the good and the bad, the joys and the disappointments.[62]

Most people soon discover that relationships in real life are quite a wake-up call compared to the false impressions and false intimacy offered online. Until a man recognizes that he will only be fulfilled with true intimacy, as God has designed for us, his search will continue from one disappointing pseudo-relationship to another.

Yet, the clear biblical recipe for well-being is a lifestyle of real life-on-life intimacy with God and others. Before Adam and Eve sinned, they were naked and felt no shame (Gen. 2:15). This is a picture of comfortable, authentic intimacy between God, Adam, and Eve. After their sin, they hid from God and one another.

Clearly, God's ideal continues to this day. He paid the ultimate price of the blood of His son to remove the sin that separates us from true intimacy with Him and one another.

He longs to reveal Himself to us that we might know Him (see Eph. 1:17; Col. 2:10; Phil. 3:10) and has removed the barriers constructed by our sin, that we might know one another and be perfectly joined in unity (see 1 Cor. 12:24–26; Eph. 2:14–18; 4:25). He calls us to love as He has loved us, with a self-sacrificing commitment to authentic relationships (see John 13:34, 35; Col. 3:12–14; 1 Peter 3:8; 1 John 4:7–11).

A few years back, I was on a private study retreat near Mount Lassen in Northern California. I had been alone and out of touch from everyone for three days. Something (I cannot remember what, because there was no television or Internet) stimulated lustful thoughts and temptation that night. I was feeling a strong and unusual temptation to settle for a quick fix. But throughout the day, I had been reading about intimacy with God. I had studied in previous days about this issue of false intimacy. At that moment, God gave me a special dose of grace.

In the late-night quietness of the bedroom, I laid on my back, spread eagle, facing the dark ceiling. And I cried out to God with a tearful prayer that went something like this:

> Oh Father, I give myself to You and You alone to meet
> my deep need for intimacy. Only You satisfy. Come right

now and let me know Your deep and unconditional love for me. I draw close to You in intimacy as you draw close to me. Lavish Your love upon me as I give my love to You. Romance me with Your unconditional acceptance and embrace of grace. Let me know, enjoy, and experience You with my entire being.

That was a powerful moment as I listened to His quiet call to intimacy with Him through His full provision in the Lord Jesus. This is real intimacy. It empowers a man to experience true self-giving love with others.

Don't settle for cheap substitutes of ink-dot images or video screen counterfeits. There is something much better and He calls you to it and to Him every minute of every day.

## Positive Truth
## Reason #24

By learning the relational skills of authentic intimacy, I can enjoy God, others, and life to the fullest.

# 25

# I avoid future mental, emotional, and spiritual scars on my life.

**'VE MARRIED** a lot of scarred people. Of course, on their wedding day, they look spectacular. The groom's hair is nicely cut; he's clean-shaven and sporting a stylish, classy tux. And the bride—wow! She looks angelic in her white gown with hair fixed elegantly and a beautifully made-up face. They've never looked better—on the outside.

But I've known all too well that as they stand there pledging their vows, most bear some pretty ugly scars on the inside. You know, pastors talk about these things with people over the years. Premarital counseling tends to reveal some of the scars. Statistics tell us the rest of the story.

I've known many couples who wished they could go back and retrieve their virginity, but that balloon only pops once. I've known scores of grooms who are ashamed of sexual escapades. After the honeymoon, I've revisited couples who struggle with intimacy and communication. The common thread in many of these scenarios is a connection to porn.

Of course, the scars surface at other times in life's journey. I've prayed with brand-new Christians, still in their teens, but regretful over the damage that pornography has caused in their homes and their hearts. On the other end, many an older man has sat in a prayer circle regretful over wasted years of slavery to lust.

Over the years I've accumulated an extensive system of reference files. In my pornography folder, I recently found the drawing of a tree. I am not sure who created it but the trunk of the tree is labeled pornography. The branches are also labeled, indicating the potential fruit of porn. The branches are prolific: Death of Innocence, Rape, Molestation, Sexually Transmitted Diseases, Promiscuity of Young People, Abortion, Prostitution, Child Prostitution, Vulgarity, Sexual Harassment, AIDS, Domestic Violence, Affairs, Incest, Homosexuality, and Divorce and Marriage Breakdown.

> I've learned that our mistakes and hurts in life begin as an open wound. They progress into a tender scab. Through Christ, they can eventually become an empowering scar.

That's quite a collection of potential scars. You may or may not see the direct correlation between pornography and each item on the tree. However, I would guarantee that most credible counselors could easily connect the dots.

It's really not rocket science. The consequences are real. The pain is massive. The scars are damaging and enduring. The best way to avoid the bitter fruit of the branches is to cut down the tree.

Shel Silverstein in his book, *Where the Sidewalk Ends,* wrote of a fictional character that wandered through some swamplands and was bitten on the toe by a mysterious little creature called a Yipiyuk. The little predator persisted and would not let go. After years of coaxing, yelling, crying, and negotiating, the Yipiuk still held its grip. The frustrated character in the poem laments the fact that after sixteen years, he still must drag the Yipiyuk everywhere he goes. The poem ends with the explanation that at last the reader now knows why Silverstein's fictional character walks so slowly.[63]

We never know what might bite us as we wander through the swampland of pornography. The persistent Yipiyuk reminds us that mysterious burdens attach themselves to the heart, mind, and lifestyle of the swamp-wanderer. Even though we may not understand the nature of how it happens, the fact remains—a simple meandering through the swamp of pornography can impede our spiritual, mental, and social well being for many years to come.

The Yipiyuk can also represent the temptations you're always fighting against or a bad habit or lustful thought you may already have. If the character in the poem had not been wandering through the swamp, he would not have met the Yipiyuk. In retrospect, he should have stayed out of the swamp.

In an earlier chapter, we noted Dr. James Dobson's interview with serial killer Ted Bundy prior to Bundy's execution. Reflecting back on that interview, Dobson commented:

> Although many people are able to view pornography without following Bundy's murderous path, *few are able to escape the mental and emotional scars that change their view of sexuality and jeopardize their ability to have normal relationships* (emphasis added).[64]

If you are just now wading into the swamp of porn (or even thinking about it), the goal of this chapter is to help you avoid unnecessary mental, emotional, and spiritual scars. Keep the Yipiyuk off your toe altogether.

If you're already dragging the Yipiyuk of porn pain, the goal of this chapter is not to leave you defeated by regret. Regret is a needless waste of emotional resources. To wallow in the slimy wasteland of regret is incredibly defeating.

My heart would be that you not wallow, but worship. Worship Jesus the Savior, the only One who can remove regret and transform it to holy desire. He can forgive and cleanse. By His wounds, your wounds can be healed.

I've learned that our mistakes and hurts in life begin as an open wound. They progress into a tender scab. Because of Christ, they can eventually become an empowering scar. Let your life become a trophy of His grace, not a story of disgrace. He alone can keep us from the scars of sin. He alone has the power to help us begin again.

## Positive Truth
## Reason #25

I can escape misery and truly enjoy life when I avoid the mental, emotional, and spiritual scars that inevitably come through pornography.

# 26

# I experience the joy
# of the Christian life.

**A**UTHOR **C. S. LEWIS** noted that "joy is the serious business of heaven."[65] Our God is a God of profound joy. In fact, joy is standard operating procedure for the believer.

Joy is that deep, abiding sense of well-being provided by the Holy Spirit, in spite of the circumstances of life. This joy is maintained through an obedient, Spirit-controlled lifestyle. It is undermined through disobedience and broken fellowship with God.

The old acrostic for joy has become so commonplace that we've almost forgotten its

> God's plan is to demonstrate the joy of His life in and through us. No artificial ingredients are necessary.

power. Jesus. Others. Yourself. JOY. The reality is important. Joy springs from a Christ-centered, others-focused orientation. The Lord's character of joy must be our preoccupation. I've heard it said that He is the happiest being in the universe. In response to Him, our vision for joy and vitality in joy will grow. Giving ourselves for the joy of others increases our joy, theirs, and His.

The primary hindrance to joy is a preoccupation with self. You could easily conclude that sin is the primary joy-drainer because it is a complete consumption with self. As we've reiterated already, porn is ultimately selfish and excludes joy.

Without the presence of real joy in our lives, we are left with artificial tactics. The plastic smile. Trying to get pumped up through the things around us, whether those things are sports, people, tasks, or other diversions. God's plan is to demonstrate the joy of His life in and through us. No artificial ingredients are necessary.

After King David repented of his adultery and murder, he was able to write these words:

> Let me hear joy and gladness;
> Let the bones you have crushed rejoice. . . .
> Restore to me the joy of your salvation
> and grant me a willing spirit, to sustain me.
> Then I will teach transgressors your ways,
> and sinners will turn back to you
> (Ps. 51:8, 12, 13).

It's fascinating that the recovery of joy was so central to his desire for renewed wholeness. In this new "joy mode" came a fresh willingness to follow, a new sense of endurance, a focus on helping others. No doubt, joy is the preferred mode for living.

After he was restored to the Lord, he stated:

> Yes, what joy for those
> whose record the LORD has cleared of sin,
> whose lives are lived in complete honesty! (Ps. 32:2 NLT).

God has the power to deliver us from porn. Of course, He does so in conjunction with our decisions to "think before we look," leading to a pattern of purity. This deliverance from the spiritual enemy of pornography results in the same joy as the psalmist describes:

> Then my soul will rejoice in the LORD and delight in his salvation. My whole being will exclaim, "Who is like you, O LORD? You rescue the poor from those too strong for them, the poor and needy from those who rob them" (Ps. 35:9, 10).

Joy is good for us and for others. It is an essential counterpart to living a life of well-being and positive influence. As we think and walk, beyond the joy-killer of porn, we can truly say, the joy of the LORD is my strength (Neh. 8:10).

---

### Positive Truth
### Reason #26

Because God wills it, I want it, and others need it,
I can commit to experience the joy of the
Christian life as I walk in daily purity.

---

## 27

# I lay up eternal rewards.

**N THE NINETEEN** years of my formal education, I learned a lot of facts. Just as important, I picked up many lessons about life. One valuable nugget came as I began to realize that even though I often lost track of my performance in a class, the teacher did not. I may have forgotten about previous absences. I may not have been keeping tabs on my grade in a particular course. The details of my test and quiz scores, the grades on all my papers, and the assessment of my classroom conduct all seemed to blur together for me. But every detail of my academic performance was clear as a bell to my professors. And at the end of my four years of college or three years of seminary, the records office had an accounting of every academic move I had made. It all came out in a very precise grade point average.

Life can be much like that. It all seems to blur together. We can begin to think that no one is really keeping track of the details of our decisions and behaviors. If we forget the finer points of our days, who else is going to care or remember?

Here is a reality check.

Therefore we are always confident and know that as long as we are at home in the body we are away from the Lord. We live by faith, not by sight. We are confident, I say, and would prefer to be away from the body and at home with the Lord. So we make it our goal to please him, whether we are at home in the body or away from it. For we must all appear before the judgment seat of Christ, that each one may receive what is due him for the things done while in the body, whether good or bad (2 Cor. 5:6–10).

Here's another reiteration of the same truth:

For we will all stand before God's judgment seat. It is written: "As surely as I live," says the Lord, "every knee will bow before me; every tongue will confess to God." So then, each of us will give an account of himself to God (Rom. 14:10–12).

Paul reminds us that we are living *in* one world but *for* another. Our focus and preference is supposed to center on the world to come. Our cur-

> Eternity honors and rewards your daily decisions to serve your Lord above your lust.

rent existence is a vapor that appears for a moment then vanishes. The next world lasts forever. So, we live by faith (a focus on the unseen) rather than by sight (the sensations and appearances of the here and now). Our ambition and goal is to please Him.

Why? Because, like our teachers in school, He is keeping track of it all, even if we aren't. We will all give an account of what we have done while on this earth in our physical body. That's riveting.

However, for the Christian, this judgment is not a judgment of our sin. All of our sin has been forgiven by the blood of Christ and we are declared righteous in Him. The judgment seat of Christ is all about rewards, lost and gained.

Living in sin rather than obedience robs us of our reward. Even doing the right things but for self-serving reasons robs us of our reward. Living to His honor in a life of loving trust and surrender brings great eternal reward.

One more pastoral note. People often wonder about the nature of our rewards. I believe our reward in eternity will involve our capacity to bring glory to Him in the ages to come. Our rewards are pictured as *crowns*. As you may know, in heaven, we cast our crowns at His feet in worship (Rev. 4:10).

What does this have to do with last night's visit with Web page Wanda? You may not think about the ways in which you are flushing your eternal rewards down the toilet, but He is. You may not realize all of the rewards you are abdicating by living in disobedience, but He does.

On the positive side, you may not understand the eternal value of your resistance to temptation and your choices to live in His Spirit, but He sees it and He remembers it. He keeps track of every "cup of cold water" given in His name. I believe eternity honors and rewards your daily decisions to serve your Lord above your lust. I believe He is delighted when you abstain from sexual sin and remain useful to the Lord and others through a life of holiness.

Ray Boltz brought living color to this idea in his classic song, "Thank You." The lyrics describe people coming up to Him in eternity with gratitude over the sacrifices made on earth that resulted in changed lives. Someday we will want others to come up to us with gratitude in their hearts because of the way our pure and purposeful lifestyles made a positive, eternal impact on their earthly choices. Every time we avoid the self-serving and spiritually-draining trap of pornography, we prove ourselves useful to the Lord and are empowered to focus on the needs of others.

It is not easy to live a pure life, but it is worth it. It is worth it here on earth, and especially in eternity. Our decisions for purity will give glory to Him forever. He calls us to live by faith, not by sight or sensation. He rewards those who diligently seek Him (Heb. 11:6).

I love the story of the atheist who had a motto posted on the wall bearing the words "God Is Nowhere." His little daughter, just beginning to read, came into the room and began to spell out the phrase. She came up with "God Is Now Here." In our moments of temptation, we can fool ourselves by dismissing his presence. The reality is that He is present, paying attention and preparing a reward for the faithful.

When we hear the regular call of the porn prostitutes welcoming us to their world, we are wise to listen instead to the welcoming words we will long to hear someday from His heart: "Well done, good and faithful servant. Enter into the joy of the Lord." This perspective will fuel good decisions in the face of temptation.

I remind my congregation often that the scoreboard is in heaven. Keep your eye on that one. It's the one that counts.

## Positive Truth
## Reason #27

I can focus my energies on the eternal rewards
God has promised on the heavenly scoreboard
as I walk in integrity and purity each day.

# 28

# I learn to deal with the causes of my problems rather than treating symptoms.

**I** **F YOU HAD** a crack in your ceiling with water leaking through, you could spackle over the crack or replace a damp ceiling tile. But that wouldn't change the fact that the walls had shifted or that water was pooling over your head waiting to douse you.

If you were diagnosed with skin cancer and needed surgery, but chose instead to cover the cancerous skin with a Band-Aid, it wouldn't change the fact that you had a potentially fatal illness.

If you had an employee who was regularly stealing money from your company and you kept putting your own money into the register so that the balance came out right at the end of the day, it wouldn't change the fact that someone in the organization was ripping you off.

If you struggle with pain from your past or are unable to relate to others in an authentic way or cannot cope with your stress and decide to find escape and release through pornography, it does not solve the issues of your life.

In fact, superficial attempts to relieve the symptoms of a problem usually make things worse. The leaky ceiling drips more. The skin cancer spreads. The thieving employee gets wealthier at your expense. The issues that drive our interest in pornography deepen over time.

Experts agree that pornography and masturbation are most often an attempt to mask pain and relieve frustration. Rather than solving the source of the problem, a man simply extends the symptoms. Compounding the difficulty is the fact that pornography is so addictive and can lead to even more pain and a deeper withdrawal from reality.

In his book *False Intimacy*, Dr. Harry Schaumburg offers some real solutions. He challenges the sexually addicted person to:

+ face yourself honestly without denial
+ recognize your need to change

> Superficial attempts to relieve the symptoms of a problem usually make things worse.

+ face your woundedness
+ realize you cannot heal yourself and turn to God
+ trust God to satisfy your needs
+ acknowledge your need of repentance
+ confess your sins before God
+ ask for help
+ pursue healthy relationships
+ receive a physical examination
+ consider joining a support group
+ recognize that change is a process[66]

Regardless of where a man lands in the addiction cycle, every one of us can glean from this advice. By turning away from pornography and choosing a pathway of real life change, we develop new patterns of problem solving. We learn to manage the power of our sexuality in a way that creates wholeness rather than deeper woundedness. Honest recognition, humble admission of need, looking to the Lord, and opening your life to the help of other godly people are vital. This is a process that can be long and tedious—but it is worth it.

Even King David, a man after God's own heart, following months of denial and treating symptoms (like killing Uriah, his mistress's husband) came to a point of true life change. Through a bold prophet, a message of truth, and a response of self-honesty, David finally began to address the issues of his heart. You can read all about it in Psalm 51. To me the core turnaround truth is found in verse 6: "Surely you desire truth in the inner parts; you teach me wisdom in the inmost place."

Denial and superficial treatments make for a miserable existence. At the end of the day—and the end of the road—we all want to look back knowing that we have addressed our issues honestly and thoroughly for the sake of our own character, for the good of others around us, and to the glory of God.

### Positive Truth
### Reason #28

I will learn to deal with the causes of my problems in pursuit of a sincere and secure life while refusing a superficial treatment of painful symptoms.

# 29

# I prevent potential temptations for others in my sphere of influence.

**O**NE RAINY AFTERNOON I had just finished my college classes and was hurrying to get to the parking lot. A street separated my classroom and my car. Carelessly, I sprinted into the road and did not even notice an oncoming car to my right. I quickly stopped in my tracks before crossing the median. Too late. I had startled the driver. Because the street was wet and on a steep decline, her car began to skid as she hit her brakes. Before I knew it, she slammed right into a telephone pole on the far side of the street. Technically, I never crossed the line to her side of the road. However, it was obvious that my inattention had caused her accident. As you might guess, I felt horrible about the incident.

Carelessness is the impetus to many costly mishaps in life. Over a hundred thousand unintentional injury deaths occur annually in the United States. It is the fifth leading cause of death after heart disease, cancer, stroke, and chronic respiratory disease.

The economic impact of all unintentional injuries (fatal and nonfatal) in 2003 was $586.3 billion, which works out to be $2,100 per capita or $5,600 per household. Besides the $586.3 billion in economic losses (which includes employer costs, vehicle damage, fire losses, wage and productivity loss, medical expenses, and administrative expenses), lost quality of life is valued at $1.272 trillion, bringing the total comprehensive cost to $1,858.3 trillion.[67]

Engaging in pornography can be pretty careless behavior. I've spoken with many men who were introduced to pornography as boys because a careless adult left it lying around or disposed of it inadequately. It may have been at a friend's house or lying on top of a trash can. Ted Bundy was first exposed to porn by rummaging through some carelessly discarded trash behind his home.

> I am not only accountable for the intent of my actions, but also for the impact of my actions on others.

With the proliferation of porn on the Internet, it has become even easier for others to encounter it. Web pages visited, cookies deposited, and unwanted spam linked to spyware all pose potential exposure to others.

Jesus offered some unyielding warnings about the matter of causing others to stumble.

> But if anyone causes one of these little ones who believe in me to sin, it would be better for him to have a large millstone hung around his neck and to be drowned in the depths of the sea. Woe to the world because of the things that cause people to sin! Such things must come, but woe to the man through whom they come! (Matt. 18:6, 7).

Over the years I have learned that I am not only accountable for the intent of my actions, but also for the impact of my actions on others. Avoiding pornography and eliminating every hint of it from your life may prevent untold heartache to a handful or even hundreds of others.

Paul serves as a great example to us all. His heart should become our heart. He wrote, "It is better not to eat meat or drink wine or to do anything else that will cause your brother to fall" (Rom. 14:21). To the Corinthians he said, "Therefore, if what I eat causes my brother to fall into sin, I will never eat meat again, so that I will not cause him to fall" (1 Cor. 8:13).

Because your life is inevitably interconnected with others, you do well to avoid throwing stumbling blocks in their pathway through hidden habits and stashes of steamy smut. This is just another great reason to pursue complete purity.

## Positive Truth
## Reason #29

I will consider and value others by preventing any potential pornographic temptations that might hinder or hurt them.

## 30

# I honor the trust and prayer support of those who have invested in my spiritual life.

THE 1995 FILM *Waterworld* portrayed a futuristic world in which the polar ice caps had melted and humanity was forced to live upon the oceans. Dry land was regarded as a myth, and even a handful of dirt had become the equivalent of gold.

By the time of its release, a lot of gold had been invested in the film. Reliable estimates placed the cost at $170 million to $180 million (although some estimates were as high as $350 million). To date, this was almost twice the figure of the world record for the previous most highly budgeted film and higher than the gross national products of several African nations.

Without a doubt, the film was a misguided investment of epic proportions. The film needed to outsell *Jurassic Park* (1993) simply to break even. Even if it became one of the top ten box-office successes of all time, it still stood to result in a massive financial loss.

In the process of filming, there were additional price tags. Kevin Costner's marriage broke up following his fling with a dancer he worked with during filming. The film's multimillion-dollar set collapsed during a hurricane. Director Kevin Reynolds was fired during the last weeks of shooting. Costner was forced to take over the director's chair in an effort to save the film.

The film grossed around $88 million and proved to be one of the worst investments in film-making history.

*Waterworld's* misfortune was so remarkable that an episode of *The Simpsons* featured an amusing satire with a *Waterworld* video game that cost forty quarters for thirty seconds of playtime.[68]

It is wise for us to remember that pornography can turn our life into a real-life *Waterworld*. Too many people have invested in us for our journey to end in disaster. The bondage of porn puts their generous investments of prayer, time, money, and love at risk.

A wise investment manager is tuned in to the wishes and desires of his investors. Your life is the result of many loving investors who have sacrificed significantly for your success.

> **Your life is the result of many loving investors who have sacrificed significantly for your success.**

Next time the porn queens call your name, turn up the volume on the voices of your investors. Think of your mother cheering you on. Let her voice remind you of her love and sacrifice on your behalf. You certainly would not want your mom catching you indulging in girly magazines.

If you had a good relationship with your father, listen to him urging you to make wise choices. Hear the supporting encouragement of the ones who led you to Christ, taught your Sunday school classes, or discipled you in the faith.

Remember the investment of schoolteachers, pastors, or work supervisors who have supported you in so many ways. Consider the many friends who have helped you, encouraged your faith, and bolstered you in tough times. Certainly there are other family members who have sacrificed time, money, and prayers on your behalf. Picture them all right now in the stands as you run your race of life. They love you and want the very best for you. They also want a good return on their investment and would not be happy with your high-risk romps through pornland.

I think of biblical examples of the power of personal investment and how it inspired the recipient to the high ground of moral excellence.

Jesus invested much in Peter. In spite of his failings, Jesus was determined to do well on His investment in His disciple. Jesus told him, "Feed my sheep." Peter went on to lead the early church in evangelistic impact that brought thousands into the kingdom. He was faithful to the end, dying a martyr's death.

Paul poured his life into Timothy, and urged him to press on fearlessly in the face of opposition. He charged Timothy, "And the things you have heard me say in the presence of many witnesses entrust to reliable men who will also be qualified to teach others" (2 Tim. 2:2). Paul envisioned a faithful finish for Timothy, one that would impact coming generations with the truth.

A lot of people have invested in you. Consider the privilege of the gifts of love, support, and sacrifice you have received. Make them proud. Put away the porn and faithfully embrace the high road of purity.

## Positive Truth
## Reason #30

I will honor the trust and prayer support of those who have invested in my spiritual life as I walk in the path of purity and integrity, paved by their example and care.

# 31

# IF I AM MARRIED

## I avoid adultery in my heart.

**O**NE OF THE great myths many men believe is that getting married will solve their problem with pornography and masturbation. Men think that once the real thing is available all the time, the need for the artificial will fall away.

Many men have been baffled by their continued struggle even after marriage. They love and enjoy their wives, but for reasons beyond their comprehension they are still straying with their eyes and actions.

Of course, the cause of lust is not one's marital status. While it is better to marry than to burn, the burning does not necessarily find full satisfaction in one's wife unless the core issues driving the behavior are addressed.

In fact, sometimes the problem becomes worse after marriage. I know it sounds crazy to an unmarried guy, but it is true. Much of the struggle with porn and masturbation is a search for intimacy driven by pain, disappointment, or stress. After marriage the relational stakes increase. Unresolved pain in the relationship, disappointment with the wife's sexual responsiveness, and the stress of running a household can all compound the issues.

Instead of resolving their resentment through prayer, communication, reconciliation, and servanthood, many married men justify increased wandering. They resort to porn to get what they feel their wife is unwilling to offer. They channel their anger to find satisfaction in images rather than pursuing real intimacy.

A married man might consider what he would do if his wife became ill or handicapped and could no longer satisfy his sexual urges. Would this be a justification for porn? Or would he have to develop ongoing intimacy without sex—and trust the Lord to give him grace for his drive by providing the natural outlets during his sleep?

One thing is for sure: the stakes of playing around with pornography are higher once you are married. For one, a man is now in a covenant relationship with his wife and pledged to sexual fidelity. Should children grace the home, the implications are even more serious.

For the married man, every mental sexual escapade is adulterous. Let's review the obvious passage:

> You have heard that it was said, "Do not commit adultery." But I tell you that anyone who looks at a woman lustfully has already committed adultery with her in his heart. If your right eye causes you to sin, gouge it out and throw it away. It is better for you to lose one part of your body than for your whole body to be thrown into hell. And if your right hand causes you to sin, cut it off and throw it away. It is better for you to lose one part of your body than for your whole body to go into hell (Matt. 5:27–30).

Jesus makes it clear that adultery is more than jumping in the sack with someone other than your wife. It begins in the heart—and God sees the heart and knows our imaginations and intentions.

Further, Jesus makes it very clear that every man must be responsive to the truth and responsible for his actions, even to the point of taking radical measures to avoid the path of a wandering heart. This passage is not literally teaching self-mutilation. This would violate the biblical teaching on the sanctity of the body as a temple (1 Cor. 6:19, 20). But He is making it very clear: do whatever you have to do to stop sinning by lusting.

I have another list called "40 Reasons Why I Do Not Want to Commit Adultery." I wrote it many years ago after I followed a pastor who had left the church due to a long-term affair. Seeing the destructive fallout from his actions helped me think of reasons to avoid that tragic path.

> One thing is for sure: the stakes of playing around with pornography are higher once you are married.

Do whatever you have to do. Review the consequences. Arrange your life to stay away from the places and times when you tend to be tempted. Get into some accountability with a brother who will stay close and ask the hard questions.

Water your grass. Keep the marriage close and consistent through regular prayer, communication, and activity together. Go to a Christian counselor to work out issues that prevent intimacy. Most of all, keep an authentic relationship with the Lord. Ultimately it is your love for and obedience to Him that will keep you from the path of adulterous thought patterns and behaviors.

Be honest about the fact that it could happen to you so that you are realistic in guarding your heart and lifestyle as a couple. Statistics vary greatly, but on the low end estimates are that 25 percent of wives and 44 percent of husbands have had extramarital sex.[69] Another study indicates that 66 percent of women and 68 percent of first marriages have had an affair.[70]

In any case, the possibilities are real, the temptations are rampant, the broken marriages are abundant, and the need to keep watch over your heart is urgent.

Focus on the positives that come with faithfulness of heart and action toward your wife. As a pastor, I've been blessed to conduct many vow renewal ceremonies and attend a lot of major anniversary celebrations. There is nothing more beautiful than a couple who have been married fifty years. Their love has become amazingly real and deep. They've stayed on task with the hard work of developing intimacy and companionship. They are surrounded by friends who respect them. The admiration of their children and grandchildren is profound. Most of all, they are an incredible tribute to the goodness, faithfulness, and grace of God.

You may never make fifty years due to a late marriage or a previous broken marriage. But live every day with that vision in mind. The blessings are yours for the taking as you steer clear of the affairs of the mind and heart that seek to trip you up through porn.

## Positive Truth
## Reason #31

By avoiding adultery in my heart, I will demonstrate genuine love for the Lord and my wife.

## 32

# I encourage my wife's trust.

**T**RUST IS a fragile thing. It takes years to build and just one breach of character to damage. Of course, through a commitment to honesty and consistency, blended with a strong dose of forgiveness, it can be restored over time. Still, the better road is to live in a trustworthy way every day. A good choice to this end is to avoid porn.

Few things can undermine your wife's trust more quickly than a pattern of playing with pornography. Not only does it hurt her in significant ways, but it reveals a pattern of secrets and lies.

One woman whose marriage and family had been deeply affected by pornography said it pretty directly:

Most sex addicts are pathological liars. They lie about everything, not just their sexual behavior, and they do so with straight faces. They lie when telling the truth would save them time and money. They lie about little things as well as big ones. They lie to themselves about what they're doing. They lie to their wives and families about where they're going and what they're going to do when they get there, even if there's no sexually inappropriate behavior going on. Pornography itself is a lie, and they embrace it.[71]

Keith Intrater in his book *Covenant Relationships* offers this insight: "Sin then, is the breaking of the trust of another person. One cannot sin in the abstract. Sin is not the failure to accomplish a certain action. Sin is personal, and sin is relational."[72]

It is wise for the struggling husband to put some warning signs along the entry ramp to porn. One important reminder is the fact that every journey into the lust-filled fantasy land is a violation of your wife's trust. How so?

> "Sin then, is the breaking of the trust of another person. One cannot sin in the abstract."

Your wife trusts you to take care of her, to love her, and to desire her. She trusts you to tell her the truth and relate to her in honesty. She trusts you to let her into your life and struggles as she does the same for you. Porn undermines all of these important factors in your relationship.

Over time, it does not take too many violations of trust to completely undermine her ability to trust. When a marriage is devoid of trust, it lacks the necessary foundation for survival.

If you've already violated your wife's trust, it is imperative that you stop the lifestyle of lies that is inherent in porn use. Otherwise, you will dig the ditch deeper each day. Repent. Get professional help. Do whatever you have to do to demonstrate that you are sincere about changing.

Commit to honesty from this moment on. Make your life an open book to her in every way—including your use of the computer, your spending, your reading, etc. Over time, trust can be restored.

When the Babylonian underlings had become jealous of Daniel's favor with the king, they sought to find charges against his conduct. But the Bible says, "They could find no corruption in him, because he was trustworthy and neither corrupt nor negligent" (Dan. 6:4). This example can inspire you in your walk with the Lord and your life before your wife.

Proverbs 20:6 and 7 honors a man worthy of trust when it declares, "Many a man proclaims his own loyalty, but who can find a trustworthy man? A righteous man who walks in his integrity—How blessed are his sons after him" (NASB). Trust produces great blessings in your marriage and for your children.

George MacDonald said, "Few delights can equal the mere presence of one whom we trust utterly. To be trusted is a greater compliment than to be loved." Ralph Waldo Emerson noted, "Man's life would be wretched and confined if it were to miss the candid intimacy developed by mutual trust and esteem." Let's make it a goal to rediscover this delight as we put the problem of porn behind us.

## Positive Truth
## Reason #32

By avoiding pornography I will encourage my wife's trust and enjoy the countless benefits that come with it.

## 33

# I honor my vow of marital purity and faithfulness.

**N**O DOUBT, AMERICANS have lost a sense of the power of a marriage vow. It seems that for many of us, marriage has become more of an experiment in social fulfillment than a lifetime commitment for better or for worse.

Sadly, high-profile vow violations are all too common. Of course, marriage is as disposable as a shaving razor in Hollywood. The sexual escapades of President Bill Clinton set a new low in the credibility of the marriage vow. Many were troubled when Christian artist Amy Grant and her new beau Vince Gill disposed of their current spouses to take new "vows."

In 2000, U.S. House Speaker Newt Gingrich dumped Marianne, his wife of nineteen years, shortly after quarter-backing a conservative contract with America. Apparently part of the contract included the freedom to shack up with a young congressional aide for seven years.

We've all been jolted by George Barna's figures indicating that professing Christians have moderately higher rates of divorce than the general population, including atheists and agnostics.[73]

The discarding of marriage vows does not begin in a hotel room or back office. It begins in the mind and heart. Playing with porn constitutes a significant dismissal of the pledge of fidelity, endurance, and faithful dedication.

Maybe Rep. Barney Frank, D-Mass., got it at least half right when he complained, "They're saying that my ability to marry another man somehow jeopardizes heterosexual marriage. Then they go out and cheat on their wives. That doesn't jeopardize heterosexual marriage?"[74]

This is precisely what William Bennett, author of *The Book of Virtues*, recognized back in 1994 in a speech to the Christian Coalition's national convention: "If you look in terms of damage done to the children of America, you cannot compare what the homosexual movement has done to what divorce has done to this society. In terms of consequences to children, it is not even close!"[75]

The issue we often struggle with is that marriage involves suffering. It is one of God's most powerful character development tools and requires extreme sacrifice, willingness to change, and a lifelong commitment to put another's needs ahead of your own.

In an earlier chapter, I referred to Psalm 15. Another profound verse from that psalm states that the man of integrity "swears to his own hurt—and does not change" (v. 4). In today's society where the happiness of the individual is the core concern, we look for "change" far too quickly. Our decisions spring from a philosophy of self-satisfaction rather than a concern for the honor of God, the nature of truth, the power of one's word,

> Marriage is one of God's most powerful character development tools, requiring extreme sacrifice, willingness to change, and a lifelong commitment to put another's needs ahead of your own.

and the value of character. Instead, we should be changed as we learn to endure the sometimes difficult days of marriage. It is the bedrock belief in the honor of a vow and God's design for marriage that keeps us true.

Dr. Rick Perrin, senior pastor of Cornerstone Church (PCA) in Columbia, South Carolina, observed,

> A theology of marriage must be more than a sundry list of Scripture verses on the topic. We must develop and draw from a comprehensive understanding of God's creation of male and female, why and how "the two become one flesh" and how this "mystery," as Paul calls it, is so significant as to represent Christ's relationship with His church. If we do not live from this position, we are no different from the world around us and maybe worse when it comes to divorce.[76]

Our marriage vows are more than a ten-year, no-cut contract. They are not based on fickle feelings of happiness or passion. The vow's purity is in its permanence. The Old and New Testaments confirm this: "Man shall cleave to his wife," "The two shall become one flesh," and "What God has put together, let no man put asunder" (Gen. 2:24; Matt. 19:5, 6 NASB). Marriage is an exclusive, lifelong union.

What does this have to do with pornography? Everything. Honoring my vow starts with my private thoughts, emotions, and habits. Down the road, my wife and children will rise up and call me blessed because I had the character to keep my word, even when it hurt my emotions or self-protective interests. I will cross the finish line of this life having faithfully run the marathon of marriage with my head held high and my heart kept pure. And it will be worth it.

## Positive Truth
## Reason #33

As I avoid pornography, I honor my vow of marital
purity and faithfulness proving to be a man of
my word and true to my commitments.

## 34

# I keep my marriage union pure from fantasies of other women.

**IMAGINE YOU ARE** making love to your wife late one night. The sparks of romance are sweeter than they've ever been. She is more responsive than you can ever remember. Suddenly at the height of the moment she cries out, "Oh Charlie, you are sooo . . . wonderful. Charlie, I love you sooo . . . very much. I'm all yours!" But your name is Jim.

How would you feel? Well, this is exactly what many of us deserve. Fortunately, our wives are probably too self-controlled to say something like this, and certainly have not fueled their fantasies to the point of invading the bedroom with such bluntness.

In a section titled, "When Miss September Meets the Wife," Laurie Hall described the debilitating impact of fantasy on the marriage bed. She describes the various ways in which a husband will impose unrealistic expectations on his wife in comparison to his dream women of porn. Eventually, he can expect his wife to function as a passive, completely voluptuous sex fiend. If she is a normal wife and mother, he comes to believe that she is too controlling, demanding, independent, and frigid. In Hall's words, "She's going to be too flat, too fat, too old, or too average to suit his gourmet taste."[77]

It doesn't stop there. Men prone to sexual fantasy tend to withdraw from many of the less attractive realities of life, neglecting the everyday relationships with the spouse, children, and friends. At the same time, this man begins to think of himself as "the dominator," which is his role with women in the sexual fantasies of his other world. When passivity and domination meet, it really has a way of messing up a marriage.

One writer has observed:

> As the spiritual leaders of our homes, we're responsible for protecting our wives, not withering them. We're to honor their essence, not feed our lust. Sex with us should be as pure as prayer. We aren't to bring impurity from our past into the marriage bed: "Marriage should be honored by all, and the marriage bed kept pure, for God will judge the adulterer and all the sexually immoral" (Heb. 13:4).[78]

James 1:13–15 is an excellent description of the process and final product of fantasies:

> When tempted, no one should say "God is tempting me." For God cannot be tempted by evil, nor does he tempt anyone; but each one is tempted when, by his own evil desire (fantasy), he is dragged away and enticed. Then, after desire has conceived, it gives birth to sin; and sin, when it is full-grown, gives birth to death. (author's emphasis)

Truly, sin kills. It kills romance and reality. It kills the purity and pleasure of marriage. It kills hearts and home. Fantasy is one of its primary carriers. That is why we must keep it out of our marriage bed.

We began the chapter by imagining a romantic moment with your wife. Let's replay the same scene. Only this time, you are the one who is really hitting on all cylinders. As you and your wife are at the height of pleasure she feels some unusual movement in the bed. Looking up, she sees three other women, all Playboy bunnies, eagerly waiting their turn. You casually call them all by name and tell them you will be with them in a moment. Your wife would shriek, "I think not!"

I know we would not want to do this to the dear lady who has given up so much to support us, raise our children, and make our home such a loving and beautiful place. Let your best and only thoughts be of her.

## Positive Truth
## Reason #34

As I keep my marriage union pure from fantasies of other women, I celebrate the beauty and blessing of the very special mate God has given to me.

# 35

# I communicate acceptance and honor toward my wife.

**N**O NORMAL PERSON enjoys rejection. The feeling that you do not measure up, are inferior, and have become the brunt of someone's disdain is excruciating. If you've ever received a "Dear John" letter from a girlfriend, you know the feeling. If you've ever been turned away after a job interview, rejection is now part of your resume. If you've been cut from a sports team, you've felt the punch in the gut.

But the rejection that hurts the most comes from people we love the most, especially when it's our spouse. Far too many loyal and lovely wives have felt the devastating pain of rejection after discovering their husband's pornography habit.

In the confusion of a porn-addicted brain, the husband somehow thinks that he can still love and honor his wife, even though he is making pseudo-love to dozens of images of other women. He thinks, *It's no big deal. It's not like I am running away from her. I am still married. I pay the bills. I buy her new clothes and take her on nice vacations. She's my first love. This stuff is just entertainment.*

However, when it comes to marriage, your wife deserves your exclusive love and romance. That's the power of the marriage relationship. Unlike any other social component of our lives, it is exclusive.

When a man invites porn queens into his mind and heart, he communicates hurtful rejection to his wife. Her immediate thought is, *What's wrong with me? Why does he need to look at those other women? Why am I so inadequate? How did I get relegated to a harem of porn models?* Her questions are legit and something every husband had better be prepared to answer.

There is no way your wife can compete with airbrushed images and "girls gone wild" exhibitionism. She shouldn't. She is exactly who God made her to be—and He made her exclusively for you. She is your one and only perfect match, now that she is your wife.

Dr. Jennifer Schneider, the assistant editor of the *Journal on Sexual Addiction and Compulsivity,* speaks of the harm of porn on wives and children. She tells of one man who confessed that his addiction to pornography nearly destroyed his wife and daughter. Both women suffered from eating disorders and had suicidal tendencies because of his rejection. Every afternoon he returned from work fearing he would find his wife on the floor with her wrists slit because of her feelings of inadequacy. Years later they went through counseling and his daughter shared her struggles. Tearfully she explained her feelings of inferiority. She saw how her father totally rejected her mom, a beautiful woman, and feared never finding a man who would love her and tell her she was beautiful. The two women this man loved the most suffered greatly because their husband and father rejected them to fulfill his lust for sex.[79]

> The rejection that hurts the most comes from people we love the most, especially when it's our spouse.

First Peter 3:7 gives every husband clear marching orders on this issue: "Husbands, in the same way be considerate as you live with your wives, and treat them with respect as the weaker partner and as heirs with you of the gracious gift of life, so that nothing will hinder your prayers."

The applications are pretty obvious. Consider your wife's feelings instead of dismissing them. Be more concerned about her sense of security and acceptance than you are about your private pleasures. Her weaknesses are there for a reason—mainly to help you become the man you should be. The two of you are in this life together to share God's most gracious gifts. Don't trample them underfoot. If you do, you will not be spiritually authentic. Don't expect the Lord to listen to your prayers if you disregard the concerns and feelings of your wife. Wow. That's tough stuff—but so necessary.

A friend of mine has struggled with pornography periodically over the years. With great transparency and care, he often told his wife about the times he'd stayed up late at night looking at the scramble channel, trying to get a good look at a lusty babe.

At first it really bothered her. She was disappointed and hurt, realizing that she could not compete with the porn divas and the escapes of adult television.

The last time he confessed that he'd had a "bad night" she looked at him with disgust and simply retorted, "You wimp!" Good for her. She gets it. The problem is not hers; it's his.

Your wife may not be that tough or discerning. Still, you need to give her the honor she deserves. Accept her just as she is as your one and only lover, God's perfect gift to you. Stop wimping out. Be the husband she needs.

## Positive Truth
## Reason #35

I keep my heart free to communicate acceptance and honor toward my wife as I steer clear of pornography's disgraceful comparisons.

# 36

# I avoid the pathway that could easily result in infidelity.

**'VE COUNSELED** a lot of men who have cheated on their wives. One time I even confronted a guy at a hotel with his girlfriend. Before the night was over I spoke with them both in the hotel room, prayed with them, packed him up to take him home to his wife, and told the lady to go back to where she belonged. Wow. That was an experience.

I've never met a man who planned to get into that kind of a mess. But, in time, the intimacy of the marriage broke down and he began to put himself into compromising situations.

It does take both factors, by the way. The intimacy of a marriage can be in jeopardy, but as long as the man lives honorably, with clear safeguards in place, the marriage still has hope. But once a man starts down the slippery slope of compromise, it's a hard road to get back to where he belongs.

That's why our staff has what I call the "Ten Commandments of Leadership Conduct." They aren't all original, but truly essential:

+ Thou shalt not visit the opposite sex alone at home.
+ Thou shalt not counsel the opposite sex alone at the office.

- Thou shalt not counsel the opposite sex more than once without that person's mate. Refer them to another counselor.
- Thou shalt not do lunch alone with the opposite sex.
- Thou shalt not kiss any attendee of the opposite sex or show affection that could be questioned.
- Thou shalt not discuss detailed sexual problems with the opposite sex during counseling. Refer them to another counselor.
- Thou shat not discuss your marriage problems with an attendee of the opposite sex.
- Thou shalt be careful in answering cards and letters from the opposite sex.
- Thou shalt make your administrative assistant your protective ally.
- Thou shalt pray for the integrity of other staff members.

We need to add one more commandment, and put it at the top of the list. It will read: Thou shalt not look at pornography or fantasize in any way about members of the opposite sex.

What we imagine is what we eventually do and ultimately become. Outstanding athletes have learned to picture, rehearse, feel, and anticipate every detail of the game

> What we imagine is what we eventually do and ultimately become.

or race. The more they do this, the more instinctive an outstanding performance becomes. That power is exactly what we must avoid when it involves infidelity to our wife.

Men, we all know better. Do not think that you can tolerate distance in your marriage, then start messing with pornography and have a marriage that survives. It just does not happen.

## Positive Truth
## Reason #36

By avoiding pornography, I steer clear of
the pathway that could easily result in
infidelity and family disaster.

# 37

## IF I HAVE CHILDREN

# I minimize the risk of my children being exposed to pornography.

**R**ECENTLY I SAT down with a good friend in the ministry as we reflected on our journey in life and our interactions with pornography along the way.

He recalled the times as a young boy when he discovered his father's secret stash of *Playboys*. His dad was a dedicated Christian and church attendee. Two distinct impressions remain to this day as my colleague looks back on those days.

First, he wondered how his dad could so frequently speak of his love for his mother while lusting over the images of other women. Second, he can still recall the powerful emotions stimulated by those images, even in his preadolescent years. The feelings and imaginations stayed with him and certainly made his battle with porn much harder.

Most men who struggle with porn today were first exposed to it as children. As parents, this must be a paramount concern. If we are users, then it really appears not to be a concern at all.

Dr. Mark Laaser has written extensively on the subject of sexual addiction, even reflecting on his own struggles. As the director and cofounder of the Christian Alliance for Sexual Recovery, he addressed a committee of the U.S. Congress by saying,

> Pornography has the ability according to all psychological theory, to program children early. We are now seeing research that is telling us that, whereas in my generation of men, the average age a person first saw pornography was age eleven, now it's age five. A child who has the ability, and we're teaching them in school to do this, can get into these [internet porn] sites very easily—four, five, six, seven year olds now are seeing things that in my extensive history with pornography I never saw. Pornography that is being seen is violent. It is degrading. It humiliates people, and it's teaching our children very immature, immoral, and damaging roles about themselves.[80]

In another recent report before the U.S. Senate, Mary Anne Layden, codirector of the Sexual Trauma and Psychopathology Program at the University of Pennsylvania's Center for Cognitive Therapy classified Internet pornography as the "most concerning thing to psychological health that I know of existing today." She described the Internet as the perfect delivery system allowing for anonymity, arousal, and role models for sexual behaviors. She warned that this 24/7 household access will produce a whole generation of young addicts who will never have the drug out of their mind. Layden believes that pornography addicts have a more difficult time recovering from their addiction than cocaine addicts, since coke users can get the drug out of their system, but porn images stay in the brain forever.[81] No caring parent would want to promote this kind of addiction in their child.

Obviously this sort of exposure dramatically affects a child's attitude, sexual orientation, and sexual preferences for the rest of his life. The addictive nature of porn paves the road to various forms of acting out later in life.

Research indicates that nearly 90 percent of children ages eight to sixteen who have access to the Internet have viewed pornographic sites while doing their homework (usually in homes just like ours). Of these, 91 percent unintentionally found the offensive sites while searching the Web.[82]

The most frightening aspect of the danger of unsupervised use of the Internet is the predominance of pedophiles. Child molesters and predators use the Internet to pose as youngsters themselves to communicate with children, expose them to pornography, and arrange to meet them in person. The National Center for Missing and Exploited Children found that one in five children ages ten to seventeen who regularly use the Internet have received a sexual solicitation while online. One in four was unwillingly exposed to images of naked people or people having sex.[83]

> Most men who struggle with porn today were first exposed to it as children. As parents, this must be a paramount concern.

More than 80 percent of children who use e-mail receive inappropriate spam every day. Of all children who use e-mail, 47 percent receive spam that links to X-rated Web sites on a daily basis. Twenty-one percent of children who receive spam mail open and read it.[84]

The more a father accesses porn on the computer, the more vulnerable the entire family becomes. Embedded cookies, URL drop-down lists, and secretly downloaded spyware all open the door for porn to greet your children.

We usually think of the boys first when we consider the implications of Dad's porn problem. And it is true that sons seek to imitate the actions of their primary role model and often view women through the same lens their fathers do. But we cannot forget that daughters are also affected.

Girls shape their sense of self-worth from their father's love. Pornography in the home sends the message to young girls that women are valued only for their bodies. This belief can cultivate anger, resentment, inferiority, and fear in a woman's heart as she enters adulthood and seeks to function in marriage.

No caring father would place rat poison exposed on the kitchen counter. No loving dad would leave a loaded gun sitting in the living room. Porn is dangerous, damaging, and potentially deadly. Let's love our children by remaining spotless and pure in their eyes.

## Positive Truth
## Reason #37

Because I love my children and cherish their well-being, I will minimize the risk of my children being exposed to pornography.

# 38

# I model strong and genuine moral values for my children.

**ULTIMATELY, CHILDREN** live what they learn at home. Example is our most powerful rhetoric. Our words may tell kids what to believe, but our deeds will tell them how to live. As my children approach adulthood, I am amazed at how through them I see my attitudes, mannerisms, and behaviors staring me in the face across the dinner table. That's the way it always is.

I remember reading a story about a little girl named Ann. She was raised in a home where reading was valued but at fifteen months of age, she began to exhibit a disturbing habit. She'd pick up books, carefully turn two or three pages, then rip out the next page, throw it aside, turn a few more pages, rip out another page and throw it aside. She systematically did this with virtually every book or magazine she could get her hands on.

Her parents patiently explained to her that this was "naughty." They went out of their way to demonstrate how to treat a book with respect but to no avail. As soon as she was alone with a book, she would enthusiastically and confidently tear it apart.

Her parents were baffled until late one evening, they were relaxing, watching TV, when the mother noticed the father casually paging through a magazine that had come in the mail that day. He turned a few pages, ripped out one of the stiff advertisement inserts, threw it aside, turned some more pages, and ripped out another. The mystery was solved.[85] Children are always watching, learning, and imitating our behaviors.

Values are caught more than taught. Taking your kids to church, sending them to Christian school, and reading wholesome literature to them at home are all very good commitments. However, at the end of the day, they are watching how you live.

One of my church members tells the story of learning that while away at college, her eleven-year-old sister had discovered a pornographic magazine in her parents' bedroom. Suddenly, she remembered a similar experience when she was about the same age. She was hurt and angry to hear that her younger sibling had also been exposed to porn. While the Lord gave her grace to forgive her father, in her heart she still felt a deep sadness and sense of grief. She wrote, "I was grieving the father I had always wanted, the father I knew I would never have—a godly example and spiritual leader." She testified:

> Example is our most powerful rhetoric. Our words may tell kids what to believe, but our deeds will tell them how to live.

Dad was neither of those things, although he took us to church and even taught Sunday school. He definitely talked the talk, but stumbled greatly when it came to walking the walk. I could not respect my father, although I still chose to love and honor him as the Bible commands. But how could I respect a man who was involved in pornography? I felt disgusted; his actions made me sick, and it saddened me that I felt that way toward my own Dad. I dreaded the next time I'd see him.

Ten years have passed since that time. The siblings have engaged in very open discussions about their sex-addicted father. A couple of times, the younger brother found porn in the house and threw it in the trash. He stopped doing that because the father became very angry. The son, who was twelve at the time, was more spiritually sensitive than the father and felt he had to "protect" Dad from the evil of porn. The children also learned that Dad was first exposed to porn when he was nine years old, and it has been a stronghold in his life ever since.

This is just another sad story of the wrong kind of legacy that started with a grandfather, continued through a father, and now has deeply wounded the current generation of children.

Parents always pass to their children some kind of legacy— good, bad, or some of both.

In their book, *Your Heritage: How to Be Intentional About the Legacy You Leave*, J. Otis Ledbetter and Kurt Bruner write these challenging words:

> Today, if we don't intentionally pass a legacy consistent with our beliefs to our children, our culture will pass along its own, often leading to a negative end. It is important to remember that passing on a spiritual, emotional and social legacy is a process, not an event. As parents, we are responsible for the process. God is responsible for the product. We cannot do God's job, and He won't do ours.[86]

As you avoid pornography and all of its bitter fruit, you accept responsibility for a powerful, God-honoring heritage. You do your job and God will do His—for generations yet to come.

## Positive Truth
## Reason #38

Because my children will ultimately live what they learn at home, I will model strong and genuine moral values for my children and avoid the damage of pornography.

## 39

# I avoid embarrassing and embittering my children.

**'VE ALWAYS HAD** a special knack for embarrassing my children. My outgoing personality sometimes intrudes on the "coolness" of their existence. They are afraid their friends will view me as a nerd. They hate it when I tell stories about them. They really do not like it when I reference them in a sermon.

Sometimes my clothes are out of style. If I try to dress the way they do, I look like an old dude in midlife crisis. I often talk without utilizing some of the new jargon in their vocabulary. When I do try to use the trendier terms, I sound like an old man who is trying way too hard to relate.

But I cannot imagine the pain they would feel if I embarrassed them through some kind of scandalous behavior connected to pornography.

I remember sitting down with a young man whose father had an affair. The dad was a high-profile community leader. The newspapers had carried news stories about the scandal.

The son was devastated by his dad's violation of trust. He was angry for what Dad had done to Mom and the entire family. He was embarrassed to be identified with his defrocked father. He felt nervous about being singled out in public. It was a very distressing time in his life.

Just to keep your heart from traveling down the pathway of porn, it is good to think about how private actions could become public scandals, resulting in personal pain for people you love. If you were caught looking at porn at work, if you were caught acting out your fantasies in any fashion, or if you did something stupid to cause you to lose your job or marriage, your life would never be the same. Your relationships with your children would take a major hit.

The revelation of your hypocrisy would permanently damage the respect you have worked so hard to earn in your children's eyes. Your spiritual authority in the home would be dismantled. Future efforts to teach your children moral principles would be tainted by their anger over your inability to live by those principles.

> It is good to think about how private actions could become public scandals, resulting in personal pain for people you love.

You would become an uncomfortable topic of conversation between your children and their friends. What do they say about you? What if friends ask probing questions? It all becomes very awkward and painful.

Everything in a child wants to be proud of his dad. I remember the days of standing up to the kids down the block telling them, "My dad can beat up your dad!" We naturally want to feel secure and brave in the shadow of the strength, character, and reputation of our fathers. Don't blow it, my friend. It's not worth it.

If you have blown it or, God forbid, if you stumble down the road, own it right away. Ask your children to forgive you. Humbly admit the sinfulness of your action. By all means, get help and get past the problem. Your sincere repentance and changed life will give them hope in spite of the pain.

## Positive Truth
## Reason #39

I ultimately honor and cherish my children by avoiding the embarrassment and bitterness that could accompany a problem with pornography.

# I encourage all of the above positive qualities in their lives.

**THINK HOW EMPOWERING** it will be to your son or daughter to know that their dad avoided the temptations of pornography. Consider the advantage your children will enjoy as you experience all the benefits listed in this book. Your kids will be proud to call you "Dad." They will be inspired to know they can walk in this same victory. They will be blessed to follow in your footsteps.

A generation from now, it will be much tougher for your children and grandchildren to walk in purity. May the Lord give us all grace to face this battle head-on and create a home environment where children are encouraged to live in purity, because it is an all-out battle.

> This year, millions of children will fall prey to sexual predators. Experts estimate that one in five girls and one in ten boys in the United States are sexually exploited before they reach adulthood. These young victims are left with permanent psychological, physical, and emotional scars. That tragedy is compounded by the fact that child prostitution, human trafficking, child pornography, and international sex tourism now generate billions of dollars a year worldwide.[87]

In the face of these trends, we must do everything we can to create a home environment where wholesomeness and purity are modeled.

Recently, I read an intriguing and especially helpful report from psychologist Rob Jackson. Through counseling hundreds of sex addicts, Jackson has identified a number of common family patterns that can set up a child for addiction or at least confusion about his sexuality or relationships with the opposite sex. These patterns have to do with the attitudes that shape the spiritual and emotional climate of a home. The dangerous patterns are the following:

> Consider the advantage your children will enjoy as you experience all the benefits listed in this book. Your kids will be proud to call you "Dad."

- ◆ a home that has loose boundaries on sexual matters
- ◆ a home with overly rigid sexual boundaries
- ◆ a home filled with anger
- ◆ a home where one parent is the abandoner and the other is the enmeshed
- ◆ a home where one parent is authoritarian and the other is passive
- ◆ a home where both parents work and the children are unsupervised for long periods of time
- ◆ a home where there is a lack of respect for the children
- ◆ a home where one or both parents are involved in pornography themselves[88]

Of course, every item on that list is worth serious consideration. But don't miss that last one.

I want to leave you with a simple exercise, one I hope you will repeat often. Take a moment to review all of the previous thirty-nine reasons to avoid porn. Put your child's name in each statement. Think of how powerful it is to imagine your son or daughter navigating through this smut-filled world without succumbing to its destructive influence.

## Positive Truth
## Reason #40

Because I want to leave a legacy of honor and purity,
I will rise above the lure of pornography, planting
seeds of holiness and hope in the hearts of
my children through my example.

# Conclusion

**T**HROUGH THIS BOOK, I've done my best to equip you to win the battle against pornography one day at a time, one hour at a time, one thought at a time, one decision at a time, using one nugget of truth at a time. Let me leave you with three thoughts:

**THINK BEFORE YOU LOOK.** When an adult bookstore seems to invite you in the front door; when a magazine is calling to you from the shelf; when a link on spam e-mail tempts you to click; when the image of a voluptuous woman catches your attention out of the corner of your eye: THINK! There are forty good reasons not to look. God wants to give you preventive grace to remain on a better and purer pathway to ultimate joy and fulfillment.

**THINK AS YOU LOOK.** Sometimes you are sitting in a front row seat of sorts, looking at a beautiful woman who may or may not be dressed properly. She may be walking down the street, standing in your office, or singing on the church praise team. Let me give you the little prayer I have learned to repeat at moments like that.

> Lord, I admit, you did a really fine job on that gal. She truly reflects your beauty and creativity. However, for me

to continue to look—and lust—would be to give her the worship that only You deserve. I would steal from her things that do not belong to me. I would take from my wife the honor and love I've pledged to her alone. So I am looking away and looking to You. I love You, my wife, my children, my blessed life, and my integrity too much to waste one ounce of energy on this artificial moment of moral confusion and misguided emotion. Thank you, Jesus. Amen.

You may want to pick your own words, but I think you get the idea.

**THINK AFTER YOU LOOK.** You may mess up in the days ahead. You don't have to, but you may. Think repentance. Think confession. Think "stop it!" Review the Forty Reasons as soon as you can. Get them embedded in your being.

Trust God for grace to move onward and upward in your pursuit of purity. Someday when you stand before the Lord, you'll be glad you did. Today, when you see your children, you'll be glad you did. Tonight, when you kiss your dear and devoted wife good night, you'll be glad you did. And tomorrow, when you look at yourself in the mirror, you'll be glad you did.

# 40

# Practical Pointers for Avoiding Pornography

♦ Read your Bible daily, submitting your mind and heart to the power of God's truth.

♦ Ask God for His supernatural help each day as you seek to live in purity.

♦ Every time you struggle with pornography in any fashion, confess it immediately to God, admitting your failure and enjoying His forgiveness.

♦ Read this book completely through every month.

♦ Download the free "40 Reasons" screensaver at www.strategicrenewal. com to renew your mind about the many reasons to avoid pornography.

♦ Download the "40 Reasons" Bible studies at www. strategicrenewal.com. Use these as a companion tool for this book. Go through these in your personal time with God.

♦ Start a Bible study group and engage in these Bible studies with some other men.

♦ Get rid of all mail-order catalogues that contain seminude images.

- Ask your wife (or a roommate) to trash any of these catalogues as soon as they come.
- Do not dig through the trash looking for discarded catalogues.
- Take an 8 × 10 photograph of your family with you when you travel. Place it on top of the television in your hotel room.
- When checking into a hotel, ask the front desk to automatically turn off access to all movies.
- If you need further insulation from temptation, ask housekeeping to remove the television from your room.
- Get rid of television in your home.
- If you keep your television, do not get cable.
- If you get cable or satellite, ask your wife (or a roommate) to block all questionable stations using a password of their choice (unknown to you).
- Immediately change the channel anytime you're watching TV and something questionable happens to come on.
- Before you go see any movie, check ahead of time for nudity or inappropriate sexual content. You can do this at webpages like Screenit.com or kids-in-mind.com. Honestly, you will dramatically limit your choices in movies if you are serious about avoiding pornographic images.
- Get rid of your computer.
- If you keep your computer, locate it in an open place where others can always view the screen.
- Install software that will automatically block all questionable Web page access. I recommend Cerberian, CleanSurf, or Hedgebuilders, although many are available.
- Make sure you have your wife (or an accountability partner) control the password on these software programs.
- Download the free program called X3watch, which sends the addresses of all the Web pages you visit to an accountability partner. (Find this at www.xxxchurch.com.)
- Join the prayer team at www.xxxchurch.com and get the prayer support of others who share this struggle.
- Check out pureonline.com, an online workshop for those struggling with pornography.

- Place various pictures of your family around the computer area to remind you of your love for them and responsibility to maintain your integrity.
- Place pictures of some of the most respected people in your life around the computer.
- Put your money to work in a positive way by financially supporting ministries that are battling the problem of porn.
- Let the managers at grocery stores know that you object to the soft porn magazine covers they display at each register in full view of children and families.
- Annually, watch the *Focus on the Family* video of Dr. James Dobson's interview with Ted Bundy. This will keep you in perspective.
- Find an accountability partner and be completely honest with this person about your problem. Brainstorm about ways he can keep you accountable.
- Join a men's group where you can talk openly about this issue with prayer support and encouragement.
- Talk with a pastor at your church, seeking prayer support from your spiritual leaders.
- If your struggle is deep and potentially destructive, go see a biblical counselor right away, no matter how much time or money it takes.
- Memorize a dozen Bible verses on the subject of purity and holiness. For suggestions see the Bible study guide available at www.strategicrenewal.com. Review these weekly.
- Memorize the prayer in the Conclusion of this book. Repeat it every time an attractive woman captures your eyes.
- Read my first book, *The Seven Most Important Questions You'll Ever Answer*, in order to clarify your personal theology, identity, and purpose in life. Renewal in these truths will help keep your mind out of the gutter as you win the daily battle.
- Attend church every Sunday to experience worship with others and to have your heart challenged by God's word.
- Regularly attend a prayer group at your church, cultivating your heart for God and sharing your life with others.
- Attend a 3-Day Prayer Summit where your spiritual walk will be transformed and you can experience the deliverance of Christ.

# Notes

1. Henry J. Rogers, *The Silent War: Ministering to Those Trapped in the Deception of Pornography* (Green Forest, Ark.: New Leaf Press, 2000), p. 146.

2. John Piper, *Future Grace* (Sisters, Ore.: Multnomah Publishers, 1995), p. 336.

3. C. S. Lewis, *The Weight of Glory and Other Essays* (Grand Rapids, Mich.: Eerdmans Publishing Co., 1965), pp. 1–2.

4. John Piper, *The Dangerous Duty of Delight: The Glorified God and the Satisfied Soul* (Sisters, Ore.: Multnomah Publishers, 2001), p. 55.

5. C. S. Lewis, *Mere Christianity* (New York: Macmillan, 1952), p. 120.

6. Max Lucado, *God Thinks You're Wonderful* (Nashville: Nelsonword Publishing Group, 2003), pp. 10, 13, 14, 16, 18.

7. Bill Gillham, *Lifetime Guarantee: Making Your Christian Life Work and What to Do When It Doesn't* (Eugene, Ore.: Harvest House Publishers, 1993, reprint edition), p. 73.

8. Pearl S. Buck, *What America Means to Me* (New York: Arno Press, 1973, reprint series), ch. 4.

9. Stavros Cosmopulos, *The Book of Lasts: An Astonishing Collection of Last Acts, Last Laughs, Last Gasps, Famous Last Words, Memorable Finishes, and Other Noteworthy Endings* (New York: Penguin, 1995), pp. 18, 19, 70, 104.

10. Nathaniel Hawthorne, *The Scarlet Letter* (New York: Bantam Books, Bantam classic edition), p. 175.

11. Walter A. Elwell, ed., *Evangelical Dictionary of Theology* (Grand Rapids, Mich.: Baker Book House, 1984), p. 268.

12. *Webster's Third New International Dictionary* (Springfield, Mass.: Merriam-Webster, indexed and unabridged edition, 2002).

13. George Bernard Shaw, *The Revolutionists Handbooks & Pocket Companion*, from *Man and Superman* (New York: Heritage Books, 1962), p. 47.

14. Jan LaRue, "The Porn Ring Around Corporate White Collars: Getting Filthy Rich," issue paper for Concerned Women for America, 2002.

15. C. R. Jayachandran, "Pornography Worldwide: 260 Million Pages and Growing!" *Times of India*, September 23, 2003.

16. "Pornography Worldwide: 260 Million Pages and Growing!"

17. John Swartz and Paul Davidson, "Spam Thrives Despite Effort to Screen It Out," *USA Today*, May 8, 2003, p. 1A.

18. "NLC Summaries of 'SOB' Land Use Studies: Crime Impact Studies by Municipal and State Governments on Harmful Secondary Effects of Sexually Oriented Businesses" (Fairfax, Va.: National Law Center for Children and Families, 1979), www.nationallawcenter.org.

19. Norman Nie and Lutz Erbring, "Internet and Society: A Preliminary Report" (Palo Alto, Cal.: Stanford University Institute for the Quantitative Story of Society, February 17, 2000).

20. "The UCLA Internet Report: Surveying the Digital Future" (Los Angeles, Cal.: UCLA Center for Communication Policy, 2001), p. 84.

21. "Interview with Wordtracker founder Andy Mindel," Medium Blue, www.mediumblue.com.

22. Daniel Henderson, *The Seven Most Important Questions You'll Ever Answer* (Grand Rapids, Mich.: Discovery House, 1998), p. 209.

23. Henry Twells, "Time's Paces," poem fixed to the front of the clock case in the North Transept of Chester Cathedral in Chester, England.

24. Victoria Rideout, *Generation Rx.com—How Young People Use the Internet for Health Information* (Menlo Park, CA: Henry J. Kaiser Foundation, 2001), p. 3.

25. "Pornography Worldwide: 260 Million Pages and Growing!"

26. "Pornography Worldwide: 260 Million Pages and Growing!"

27. Michael Kirk and Peter J. Boyer (writers), "American Porn" [television series episode], *Frontline*. Public Broadcasting Service, original airdate February 7, 2002.

28. PBS Documentary, "Porn Industry Rocked by HIV Infections."

29. John Patterson, "Shocked by the torture images? Then don't miss a new documentary about the 'school' run by the US Army," *The Guardian*, May 14, 2004.

30. Richard J. Foster, *Money, Sex and Power: The Challenge of the Disciplined Life* (San Francisco: HarperCollins, 1985), p. 92.

31. Joanna Weaver, *Having a Mary Heart in a Martha World: Finding Intimacy with God in the Business of Life* (Colorado Springs, Colo.: Waterbrook Press, 2000), pp. 66–67.

32. Harry W. Schaumburg, *False Intimacy: Understanding the Struggle of Sexual Addictions* (Colorado Springs, Colo.: NavPress Publishing, 1992), p. 23.

33. Laurie Hall, *An Affair of the Mind: One Woman's Courageous Battle to Salvage Her Family from the Devastation of Pornography* (Colorado Springs, Colo.: Focus on the Family Publishing, 1993) p. 92.

34. Jim Collins, *Good to Great: Why Some Companies Make the Leap . . . and Others Don't* (New York: HarperCollins, 2001), pp. 127–128.

35. Walter Mischel, Yuichi Shoda, Monica L. Rodriquez, "Delay of Gratification in Children" *Science*, v. 244, n. 4907, pp. 933–938.

36. *Money, Sex and Power*, p. 109.

37. William J. Bennett, *The Book of Virtues: A Treasury of Great Moral Stories* (New York: Simon & Schuster, 1993), p. 47.

# NOTES

38. "New World Record for Domino Topple" Associated Press, August 18, 2003. www.cnn.com.

39. National Center for Health Statistics, Centers of Disease Control and Prevention, 2003.

40. Henry Ward Beecher, *Proverbs from Plymouth Pulpit*. Compiled by William Drysdale, 1887.

41. C. S. Lewis, *Mere Christianity* (New York: Macmillian, 1952), pp. 124–125.

42. Charles R. Swindoll, *Esther: A Woman of Strength and Dignity* (Dallas: Word Publishing, 1997), p. 41.

43. OxFam American, UN Population Fund, United States Agency for International Development. Quoted in *EMC Today* (Feb./Mar. 1993), p. 12.

44. U.S. Department of Education news release, June 30, 2004.

45. Karla Dial, "Pornography 102," *Boundless*, November 29, 2001.

46. *An Affair of the Mind*, p. 67.

47. John Eldridge, *Wild at Heart*, (Nashville, Tenn.: Thomas Nelson Inc., 2001), p. 187.

48. Stephen Arterburn and Fred Stoeker with Mike Yorkey (ed.), *Every Man's Battle: Winning the War on Sexual Temptation One Victory at a Time* (Colorado Springs, Colo.: Waterbrook Press, 2000), pp. 71–72.

49. Richard Jerome et al., "Together Again?" *People*. July 26, 2004, p. 54.

50. Dr. Victor B. Cline, "Pornography's Effect on Adults and Children," Morality in Media, 2001 <http://www.moralityinmedia.org/pornsEffects/clineart.htm> (12 December 2001).

51. Frank York and Jan LaRue, *Protecting Your Child in an X-Rated World* (Carol Stream, Ill.: Tyndale House, 2002), p. 15.

52. Jeff Olson, *When a Man's Eye Wanders* (Grand Rapids, Mich.: RBC Ministries, 1999), www.gospelcom.net.

53. Ibid.

54. Jerry Bridges, *The Practice of Godliness* (Colorado Springs, Colo.: NavPress Publishing, 1983), p. 107.

55. James R. Pomerantz, "The Grass Is Always Greener: An Ecological Analysis of an Old Aphorism," *Perception*, 12 (1983), pp. 501–502.

56. Neil Clark Warren, *Finding Contentment: When Momentary Happiness Just Isn't Enough* (Nashville, Tenn.: Thomas Nelson Inc., 1997), pp. 3–4.

57. From a letter dated March 6, 1956, in the Wade Collection at Wheaton College, Wheaton, Illinois.

58. Steven Korch, *My Soul Thirsts: An Invitation to Intimacy with God* (Valley Forge, Penn.: Judson Press, 2000), p. 9.

59. Stephen Arterburn and Fred Stoeker with Mike Yorkey (ed.), *Every Woman's Desire: Every Man's Guide to Winning the Heart of a Woman* (Colorado Springs, Colo.: Waterbrook Press, 2001), p. 61.

60. Harry W. Schaumburg, *False Intimacy: Understanding the Struggle of Sexual Addictions* (Colorado Springs, Colo.: NavPress Publishing, 1992), p. 26.

61. P. Douglas Filaroski, "Web surfing could get 'disorder' classification," *Tampa Bay Business Journal*, August 6, 2003.

62. Steve Watters, "Can Intimacy Be Found Online?" Focus on the Family, 1999. http://pureintimacy.org.

63. Shel Silverstein, *Where the Sidewalk Ends* (New York: Harper Collins, Inc. 1974).

64. *Protecting Your Child in an X-Rated World*, p. 125.

65. C. S. Lewis, *Letters to Malcolm: Chiefly on Prayer* (New York: HarperCollins, 1984, reprint edition), p. 289.

66. *False Intimacy*, pp.87–91.

67. "Injury Facts," National Safety Council, 2003.

68. Richard Scheib, "Waterworld," *The Science Fiction, Horror and Fantasy Film Review*, 1995, http://www.moria.co.nz/sf/waterworld.htm.

69. Shirley Glass, *Not "Just Friends": Protect Your Relationship from Infidelity and Heal the Trauma of Betrayal* (New York: Free Press, 2003), p. 7.

70. Annette Lawson, *Adultery: An Analysis of Love and Betrayal* (Philadelphia: Basic Books, 1988), p. 31.

71. *An Affair of the Mind*, p. 117.

72. Keith Intrater, *Covenant Relationships: A More Excellent Way* (Shippensburg, Penn.: Destiny Image Publishers, 1989), p. 16.

73. Glenn Stanton, "Divorce: Bible Belt Style," *Citizen* (June 2000), http://www.family.org/cforum/citizenmag/coverstory/a0011624.cfm.

74. Ibid.

75. Ibid.

76. Ibid.

77. *An Affair of the Mind*, pp. 100–101.

78. *Every Woman's Desire*, p. 258.

79. Jane Brody, "Cybersex Gives Birth to a Psychological Disorder," *New York Times*, May 16, 2000, p. 1, Health and Fitness.

80. *Protecting Your Child in an X-Rated World*, pp. 12–13.

81. "Internet Porn: Worse than Crack?" *Wired News*, November 19, 2004. Ryan Singel. Retrieved 1/10/2005. http://wured,cin/news/technology/0.1282,65772,00.html.

82. Cerberian, Inc. http://www.cerberian.com/02products_abusestats.htm

83. The National Coalition for the Protection of Children and Families. http://www.nationalcoalition.org.

84. "Symantec survey reveals more than 80 percent of children using e-mail receive inappropriate spam daily," *Business Wire*, June 9, 2003. Daniel L. Weiss, Retrieved 8/6/2004, http://www.family.org/cforum/fosi/pornography/facts/a0030533.cfm.

85. Jim Trelease, *The Read Aloud Handbook* (New York: Penguin Books, 2001, 5th edition), p. 38.

86. J. Otis Ledbetter and Kurt Bruner, *Your Legacy: How to Be Intentional About the Legacy You Leave* (Colorado Springs, Colo.: Chariot Victor Publishing, 1996), http://www.focusonyourchild.com.

87. "Fact Sheet: Operation Predator," July 7, 2004. www.whitehouse.gov.

88. Rob Jackson quoted by Frank York and Jan LaRue, *Protecting Your Child in an X-Rated World* (Carol Stream, Ill.: Tyndale House, 2002), pp. 86–89.

**D**ANIEL HENDERSON is the senior pastor of Grace Church of Eden Prairie, a thriving congregation of almost six thousand members in the suburbs of Minneapolis.

He also serves as president of Strategic Renewal International, a ministry dedicated to personal renewal, congregational revival, and leadership restoration.